TROLLING WITH THE FISHER KING
Reimagining the Wound

by Paul Pines

15th Cen. St. Brenden & the Stranded Whale, British Museum

CHIRON PUBLICATIONS • ASHEVILLE, NORTH CAROLINA

www.ChironPublications.com

Interior and cover design by Danijela Mijailović
Printed primarily in the United States of America.

ISBN 978-1-63051-459-4 paperback
ISBN 978-1-63051-460-0 hardcover
ISBN 978-1-63051-461-7 electronic

Library of Congress Cataloging-in-Publication Data Pending

To Carol

*

North Star
still point around which
the northern sky turns
and by which I
navigate

ACKNOWLEDGMENTS:

Essays from *Trolling with the Fisher King* appeared in the following issues of *Numéro Cinq*: "Starting in Gloucester," Vol. VI, No. 8, August 2015; "The Archaeology of Dreams," Vol. VI, No. 10, October 2015; "Constellating the Quantum Fairy Tale," Vol. VII, No. 2, February 2016 Vol; "Dinner with the Fisher King, VII, No. 6, June 2016."

I would like to thank the publisher Douglas Glover for his commitment to the project. As well as Richard Berengarten, James Hollis, Robert Murphy, Bibi Wein, Eric Hoffman, Michael Heller, Jane Augustine and Anthony Rudolph for their encouragement along the way. And my tutelary fishing guides, Claude Pines, Ted Berlin and Fred Waitzkin. My gratitude to John Peck for his close reading of the manuscript, as well as to my editor, Jennifer Fitzgerald.

I am blessed to have had in Carol, my wife, a partner whose ideas and insights have been crucial in bringing this book to fruition.

CONTENTS:

THE ARCHAEOLOGY OF DREAMS

CONSTELLATING THE NET: A QUANTUM FAIRYTALE

THE SECRET AT THE CENTER OF STONES: THE "FISHER KING FUNCTION"

<u>NOTES</u>

FOREWORD

Amfortas, the wounded Fisher King, is the mysterious figure at the center of von Eschenbach's 13th century epic, *Parzival*, and anchors the Arthurian lineage of Camelot, the Knights of the Round Table and the Holy Grail. Amfortas betrays his covenant to protect the Holy Grail by engaging in mortal combat with a Saracen knight in the name of Love. Under the banner of Amor! He kills the Saracen, but is wounded when the spear tip becomes embedded in his groin. The spear is removed but the wound will not heal. Amfortas, in constant pain, is relieved only when fishing from a skiff on a nearby lake. Hence the title "Fisher King."

The Grail that caught Christ's blood at the crucifixion—reconciles pain and love, reminds us of the importance of suffering for redemption. Carl Jung, recognizing the profound need for reconciliation, warned us that unconscious shadow material projected on to others threatens humanity as we know it. He had witnessed this first hand in the Holocaust. When his wife Emma began to explore The Grail myth, Jung promised to leave the territory to her. He kept his word. When Emma died with her book unfinished, he prevailed on Marie von Franz to bring the work to completion.

Some attention has been paid to this material. Most notably, Robert Johnson, who worked with Emma Jung, produced a compelling analysis in his book *The Fisher King and the Handless Maiden*. But specific attention to Amfortas has been surprisingly limited given the powerful implications of this figure for the post-modern world.

Trolling with the Fisher King started with my fascination with Amfortas whose original mission was to protect the container that integrated suffering and love, his inevitable distraction by the outer world and subsequent betrayal of the mission. I was drawn by the merciless condition he had to endure. His only relief from pain occurred when fishing. I had been a fisherman, and understood the comfort of this activity. As a psychotherapist, I also knew that this applied to fishing the waters of the unconscious. It appeared that we had replaced von Eschenbach's warrior culture with what Henry James called the 'Pleasure economy,' focused on entertainment, in which adolescence might be extended indefinitely. In effect, we had fled our conscious connection to the wound. It had become unconscious, and so virtually unrecognizable.

Trolling with the Fisher King

My obsession with this idea drove me to use the tools Jung had employed in his confrontation with the unconscious in *The Red Book* in the gathering of symbolic patterns and inter-disciplinary connections, to interrogate my personal experience and what I found in the world around me. I include in this my time as a fisherman, and as merchant seaman serving in the warzones of Vietnam and S.E. Asia. As a poet returning to a culture I no longer recognized, I fished for dreams, moved to upstate NY, married, raised a family, taught at the local college, earned an MSW—only to realize that the Amfortas I'd used to contextualize my condition no longer described my relationship to the wound. I embarked on a search for Amfortas in some recognizable form.

The issues Jung discussed in *Aion, Researches into the Phenomenology of the Self,* focus on the effect of cultural change on the symbolic processes of the unconscious. These remain crucial to understanding the importance of symbolic patterns, familiar imagery, and how we might find ourselves at sea in a world beyond the ability of the imagination to describe. My apprehension is that we may have already done so, that woundedness as a function appears to be increasingly disconnected from its role in becoming conscious. *Trolling with the Fisher King—Reimagining the Wound* sets off in search of the "Fisher King Function" in the hope of a hit on the other end of the line, if only to raise questions along the way. Such a journey requires a willingness to remain open to what presents itself for attention, its importance as a way of locating and perhaps redeeming what must be re-imagined. As another Fisher King on the boat, poet Charles Olson, puts it in "As the Dead Prey upon Us":

> *As the dead prey upon us, they are the dead in*
> *ourselves, awaken, my sleeping ones, I cry out to you,*
> *disentangle the nets of being!*

ADDRESSING THE WOUND

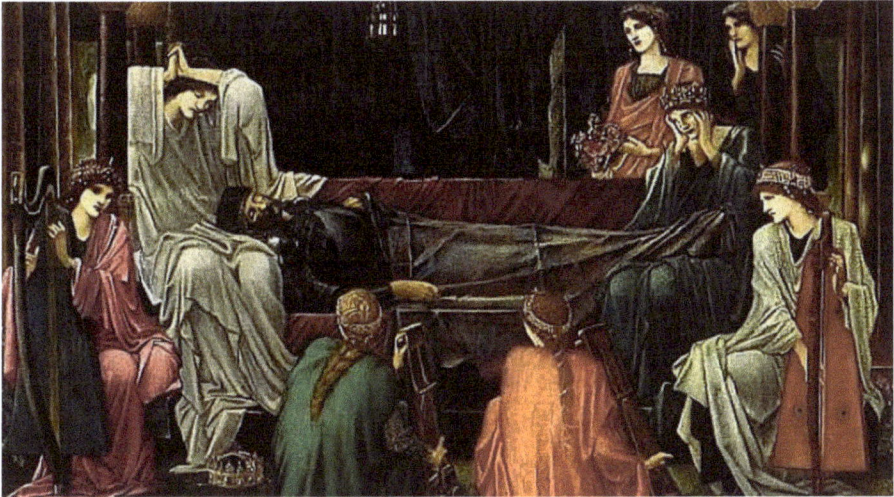

The sleep of Arthur in Avalon (detail)- Edward Burne-Jones

It is very dangerous when a wound is so common in a culture that hardly anyone knows that there is a problem.

Robert A. Johnson, THE FISHER KING
& THE HANDLESS MAIDEN

PRELIMINARY FORENSICS

My initiation into the world of Arthurian knights in search of the Holy Grail began in Brooklyn at the Patio Theater watching the 1949 movie *A Connecticut Yankee in King Arthur's Court*. I sat in the Children's Section transfixed as I watched singing mechanic Hank Martin (Bing Crosby) wake from a bump on the head in time-present to find himself in England, circa A.D. 528. Soon after, I discovered the Classics Illustrated comics version, whose cover featured a man on horseback with two guns riding against three knights in armor wielding swords. This back-to-the-future theme fired my 8-year-old imagination. Years later, what had started as a childhood fascination became a deep connection to Amfortas, the Fisher King. A central character in the Arthurian tale of *Parzival,* Amfortas betrayed his role as Grail keeper by killing a heathen knight in combat and, in the process, sustained a wound that would not heal. Speaking of *Parzival,* at 15, C.G. Jung "had an inkling that a great secret still lay hidden behind those stories."

My curiosity also led me to Mark Twain's original tale and then to T.H. White's *The Once and Future King.* As a seaman headed for the South China Sea, I read A.E. Waite's *The Holy Grail*, and later, while working the door of my Bowery jazz club, the Tin Palace, I read Mary Stewart's Arthurian trilogy starting with *The Crystal Cave.* Through much of the '70s, until the fatal recession, I thought of my club as a kind of Camelot, a beacon of light in a lawless landscape, a glimpse of transcendence for those who heard such music on the cusp of the Underworld. In the '80s, my novel *The Tin Angel* recorded my love affair with a culture that was vanishing even as I wrote about my goodbye to Camelot.

The Tin Angel garnered favorable reviews nationally, but the distributors had failed to place copies of it in bookstores. Despite despite positive critical responses, paperback edition and translations into French and German, the novel died unnoticed. Impelled by my lingering grief, I retreated into Wolfram Von Eschenbach's original tale,

Parzival, in which Herzeloyd, Queen of Waleis and Norgals, beat her own retreat into a forest cut off from the world to protect baby Parzival from the prospect of dying in battle, as had her husband and his father. Parzival ranged free, didn't even know his proper name, which means "piercing through," but responded to his mother's "precious boy" or "loving son." One day in his teens he encountered a brace of knights on horseback, mistook them for gods, followed them to King Arthur's court and vanquished the Red Knight, who blocked his way at the gate. The boy's primitive lance penetrated the knight's brain through a slit in the visor. Parzival appropriated the dead man's armor and eventually won a seat at the Round Table, becoming what his mother had feared most—a man like his father.

The tale up to this point reads like Twain's and, like a Connecticut Yankee, I made myself at home in it.. One afternoon at dusk, Parzival stopped by a lake to ask a man fishing from a skiff for directions to the nearest lodging. The fisherman, who wore a peacock plume like a crown, directed the knight to continue to a bridge, then turn left and right again. Parzival followed those directions to the Grail castle. Amfortas went on fishing. Parzival failed to recognize the wounded Grail Keeper in the fisherman whose trolling was the only thing that brought him relief. I suspected then that the Fisher King held the key to understanding what was then beyond my grasp. His wound resonated with my own unexplored wound and with the woundedness in the world around me. Unlike Parzival, I remained outside the narrative and so couldn't address Amfortas directly. I would have to come at Amfortas in another way. It never occurred to me that one day I might have to get into the skiff with him.

The Tin Angel went into paperback and was optioned by a French production company. The paperbacks were later pulped when publishers decided they no longer wanted to store inventory, and the French production was scuttled when the director became unbankable. I felt a curious sense of shame that made me think of Parzival on his way out of the Grail castle the morning after the banquet, having failed in a mission that remained unclear to him, but freighted with the consequences.

I experienced both the wound in myself and the woundedness around me as a paradoxical. On the one hand, it manifested itself in the absence of any enduring connection. As intensely as I might relate to people and places, I was just passing through. On the other hand, the pain of that condition functioned as a center without a circumference - present everywhere and impinging nowhere. It reassured me even as it begged for relief. Certain themes in *Parzival* called out to me as clues. The comfort provided by fishing and the limbic world of time at sea were foremost among them in my own experience.

GROUND ZERO

At the age of 6, I fished in Brooklyn's Prospect Park for crappies, then as a teen for blues on party boats out of Sheepshead Bay and, later, in the Bahamas for marlin. At 23, I went to sea. My abrupt departure from an NYU master's program in English the year before had left me confused. I'd felt trapped in the classroom. When I learned that the rolls had opened for applicants at the Seafarers International due to the escalation of the Vietnam War, I joined a dozen applicants at the union hall cleaning toilets, sweeping floors and emptying ashtrays for a few weeks, until the U.S. Coast Guard issued my Z-card, so called for the letter that preceded my license number, Z-11928535-D-1. I was licensed to work at entry-level deck, mess and engine room jobs.

I boarded my first ship, the *S.S. Wacosta*, in Port Newark, N.J. When I walked up the gangway on a gray October morning in 1964, duffle on my shoulder, the seaman on watch called out: "Turn around while you still have a chance!" I spent that summer in the Gulf of Mexico on deck plates hot enough to fry an egg under the midday sun. Shuttling between Beaumont, Houston, Mobile and New Orleans, I threw a line off the stern freighted with the baker's impenetrable bread, which sank as soon as it hit the water.

It was "time out of mind."

That winter, on a North Atlantic voyage, I watched a prostitute take out another woman's eye with her high heel in a Bremerhaven bar.

War Interrupted, Wayne Atherton

In front of Peter Paul Rubens' "Descent from the Cross" in Antwerp's Cathedral of Our Lady, St. John's red robe as he bore the weight of the wounded Christ buckled my knees. It seemed to me that everywhere I went, I sailed in the very wake of woundedness. In August 1965, I boarded the *Esparta,* a United Fruit refrigerator ship, in Alameda, California. The Latino crew had looped casually between Golfito, Costa Rica, United Fruit headquarters and Belize City with cargoes of bananas were shocked to find themselves now bound for the South China Sea. Once in Vietnam, the military kept us in-country as a floating refrigerator for nearly half a year. The wounds I brought back with me would fester in others as PTSD and Agent Orange. I disembarked in Seattle to find a world I no longer recognized. The advice I that I had heard on the gangway in Port Newark rang differently to me now.

"Turn around while you still have a chance!"

I secured a job in publicity at United Artists, working on films like *The Thomas Crown Affair* and *Midnight Cowboy,* but the prospect of another year picking up celebrities in limos filled me with dread. After a hot night in New York's East Village, parading on St. Mark's Place in a stifling Blue Meanie costume to publicize the Beatles' *Yellow Submarine,* I tendered my resignation.

Unwilling to go back to sea, unable to tolerate the academic or corporate worlds, I followed the brace of knights that had appeared to me as magnificent as those young Parzival followed out of the woods. These were poets like Paul Blackburn, Allan Ginsberg, LeRoi Jones, Robert Duncan and Charles Olson, who cast their lines into the deep waters of the unconscious. I began an ongoing psychotherapy at the Karen Horney Clinic for a prorated five dollars a session three days a week. To pay my way, I cruised for fares in a Yellow Cab, waited tables and tended bar.

At 32, with borrowed money, I opened a jazz club at Bowery and Second Street, The Tin Palace. It was my island of light in a war zone, and I fought to keep it alive until it fell victim to the recession. My novel, *The Tin Angel*, seemed like a passport to uncertainty. I steeled myself to continue anchorless in the drift of the world and accepted the invitation for a six-month writer's residency at a library in Glens Falls, New York. My time in the foothills of the Adirondacks turned out to be my banquet years.

Long after the light went out at my jazz club and I'd relocated from the Bowery to Upstate New York, I held onto my vision of an island of light that shines in the darkness as the centerpiece of a new life. My banquet unfolded into a loving marriage, the birth of our daughter and my midlife career as an academic. I slipped into it crabwise, teaching creative writing and literature at the local community college. This new stability encouraged me to go back to graduate school at SUNY Albany for an MSW in order to become a psychotherapist. I was the oldest student in the program, senior to most of my teachers, and the only one who approached my subjects from a Jungian point of view. In the glow of my new life, I thought of myself as one who had addressed his wound sufficiently to heal others.

My banquet played out over richly rewarding years. In contrast, Parzival experienced an intense night in a world outside of time. On arrival at the Grail castle, he was shown to his quarters, stripped of his armor and draped in new robes before being led to the banquet hall. Seated with his host, he watched maidens in procession bearing sacred objects. At the end of the parade, the Holy Grail was presented on a green cushion. Parzival noted his host's agony but felt it would be a breach of etiquette to ask about his condition. Distracted by the spectacle, under the light of a hundred candle-lit chandeliers, Parzival remained unaware of the expectation that he would heal the Fisher

King with a question that expressed concern. His mentor has taught him it was rude for a knight to question his host. He finished his meal in silence before returning to his room without understanding the pall that came over his host and those around him.

Parzival witnessed the powers of the Grail to feed everyone in the hall, but he could not heal the Fisher King. Years of wandering would pass before he had plumbed the depth of his own wound and so could return years later. My banquet rolled out over time, supported by an abundance that came without fanfare, embodied by Carol, my Queen of Cups. I moved forward too, convinced I had done what Parzival had failed to do - become who I was meant to be. My mission was to care for my family and take on the challenge of my students, with only an occasional glimpse of the kid on the gangway in Port Newark.

UNDRESSING THE WOUND

Parzival was the beating heart of the Mythology course I taught at SUNY Adirondack for 15 years. I presented von Eschenbach's tale to my students as a road map to individual growth and a guide to repairing the world. At first, they questioned how a saga written in the early 13th century, set against the backdrop of knights returning from the Crusades, could be relevant to them. I repeated Robert Johnson's point that the figure of the Fisher King represents the "wounded *feeling function*," a cultural affliction that speaks strongly to our time. While my students agreed that the consequences of such a wound could dull our ability to value and empathize with others, they argued that *Parzival* might help us understand how to address that wound.

Youth is a time when desire impregnates the natural world with promise and searches everywhere for its embodiment. As students warmed to this hero's journey, they glimpsed themselves in the mirror of the myth. Even those who had seldom read a book followed Parzival to the Grail Castle and the banquet where he failed to ask the healing question. They liked the lesson that doing what you've been told is right may, in fact, be wrong. The fact that Amfortas had been pierced through the testicles by a poisoned spear and that this wound continued to fester dogged our discussions, as did the question of why only fishing relieved his pain. Or how Parzival's shamanic transformation into the wounded healer gave meaning to the words, *What ails thee?*

Parzival played to them like a movie.

A few students referenced the film *Monty Python and The Holy Grail*, in which John Cleese plays both Lancelot the Brave and the taunting French guard whose jeers from the battlement reframe those hurled at Parzival as he left the Grail Castle. "Your mother was a hamster, and your father smelled of elderberries. Now go away, or I shall taunt you a second time."

What could be more filmic than the Grail itself, Wolfram's *lapis exillis*, a stone that glows with an inner light as messages appear on its surface then disappear as soon as they are read? My students watched it on the screen of their imaginations, creating images uniquely encoded with information about themselves. What young man or woman flipping burgers to pay for car insurance or textbooks would not be stirred by Amfortas in his fatal battle with the Saracen knight, spurring his horse as he cries, "Amour!" Or regret the Grail Keeper's choice of passion over duty as he fell wounded by a spear in his groin. My working-class students, trapped in cultural and economic limitations, recognized what it meant to be called and to yearn for it.

Years after I retired from the classroom, I continued to meet students who recall their time with Parzival and the Fisher King. Messages float back to me in emails. Unexpected encounters in banks or at the mall are often awkward, especially when they are with someone I don't recognize. Recently at the local supermarket a weathered blond woman in coveralls with an infant strapped to her chest stopped me in the produce aisle while I was looking for ripe bananas. A 10-year-old towhead was helping her push a cart full of groceries. She addressed me as "Professor." I nodded politely. Her green eyes brightened, conveying an intimacy I couldn't return. She talked about the mythology class she'd taken for a semester 10 years ago, telling me how much it had meant to her. Amfortas' suffering and Parzival's struggle with his momentous failure had helped her to make sense of the equivalents in her own life. She stroked the child's head and gazed at him adoringly, Herzeloyde (Heart's Sorrow) with her little Parzival. I wondered if in listening for the call of destiny she had understood that to suffer consciously what life dealt out was the heroic answer to that calling. She thanked me again and, with her son's help, continued to push her cart down the aisle, then turned a corner. On my way to the car I felt a warmth in my chest. As unprepared as I was for this chance meeting at the supermarket, I was equally unprepared for our parting, how much her appreciation meant and what it stirred in me.

I instantly became Parzival, pierced by my failure at the banquet, the wound I thought long healed. There was no mockery from the battlement as I walked to my car. My former student had appeared to me like a message on the Grail waiting to be read and then disappeared without telling me her name.

PREPARING THE LINES

Ernest Hemingway instructed us to write about what hurts as clearly as possible. Instead, I now find myself writing about matters of over-whelming complexity in search of what hurts.

How did this happen?

I'm not a polemicist by nature.

Indeed I have sailed through life, signing on to a variety of voyages, but not this one. Not in the twilight of my life. I had not agreed to stand at the rail trolling with the wounded Fisher King.

"Yes, you did," an inner voice challenges me. *"As soon as you boarded the Wacosta."*

"That was over 50 years ago."

"You stood in the saloon mess, looked at the Foreign Articles and put your name on the line."

"But that was not *this,*" I protest.

I bring up my banquet years, the long quiescence of my own wound and its sudden re-emergence. *How could I have been so unaware as to think I had addressed it?*

These thoughts echo those I recall when first observing Parzival's initial encounter with Amfortas at the lake. As he directed Parzival to the Grail Castle, I understood that those directions were not for me. I'd have to find my own way to address him.

"And you have."

But not until a decade after I'd stopped teaching, when I arrived as writer-in-residence at the Gloucester Writers Center, in Massachusetts, located in the former home of the poet Vincent Ferrini. The small space

Screen Man, Marc Shanker

was also haunted by Ferrini's friend Charles Olson, a giant who had left a literary footprint yet to be measured. I'd been invited here for a week to work on my poetry and give a reading from my latest collection, *Fishing on the Pole Star*. From the moment I entered, I saw and felt Olson's presence. He'd been for me like one of those knights young Parzival mistook for a god and followed out of the woods.

On my first night, I fell asleep reading Olson's signature poem "The Kingfishers," then woke the next morning disoriented, in a strange gravitational field. I seemed stuck in a place where suffering broke in waves on the shore of desire. Once again, I saw the wound in everything. Then I remembered last night's dream: Afloat on dark matter, I stood in a skiff beside a tall man in a black hoodie.

"I never signed on for this," I repeated once again.

Then the voice I now recognize as the self of my sorrow instructed me to embrace this adventure, to stop resisting and let out the lines.

DISENTANGLING THE NET

As the dead prey upon us, they are the dead in ourselves, awaken, my sleeping ones, I cry out to you, disentangle the nets of being!
"As the Dead Prey upon Us", Charles Olson

Splendor Solis – The Dark Sun

STARTING IN GLOUCESTER

1 - Pedrolino

I woke this morning in the house where the poet Vincent Ferrini lived and wrote for decades, now the Gloucester Writers Center. August 17, 2014, at 7:30 a.m., newly risen light washes purple drawstring shades, which I keep half-shut. The Cape Cod bungalow is perched on the shoulder of East Maine Street, a two-lane coastal road that runs between downtown Gloucester and Rocky Neck. Traffic up and down the hill sets up a constant rush of sound. The front door opens on a gas station/convenience store at the far side of a parking lot. In back, workmen level ground to pave a narrow alley. People walk close to the windows. There's a small kitchen at one end and a bathroom off the main room. I'll be the poet-in-residence here for a week, which culminates with a public reading from my book *Fishing on the Pole Star*.

Last night, after a chicken/vegetable stir-fry dinner, I turned on the overhead fan, moved a lamp to the side of the vintage pullout bed and perused a bookcase stacked with copies of Ferrini's collection *Know Fish*. Among them I found Charles Olsen's *Collected Works* and fell asleep reading his signature poem, "The Kingfishers." The book lay open at the foot of the bed. It reminded me of the skiff in last night's dream.

I'm in the stern fishing beside a tall man in a black hoodie: Amfortas. Not as I'd imagined him, crowned by a peacock plum. His face here, shaded by the hoodie, is entirely hidden. I hold a child's rig. The implication is clear: My rig points to an issue that limits my ability as a fisherman. I'm using puerile tools. This place, photos of its former inhabitants, our shared passion for fishing, has pulled this dream up from the sea floor.

I study images of the diminutive Ferrini next to 6-foot-8-inch Olson, the poet who mythologized Gloucester as Joyce did Dublin. Known also as Maximus and former rector of Black Mountain College,

Olson played a major role in redefining mid-20th century American poetry. Ferrini, small beside him, is no less haunting.

Vincent Ferrini, Jain Tarnower

I work on a table facing an original print of Ferrini outlined in white on a black field, dominated by his white face and hands. He wears a domed hat, like a novitiate in an obscure Italian order, but he might as easily be *Pedrolino*, the moon-faced dreamer, a stock character in the *comedia dell'arte*. His smile reads like a confidence, an intimate whisper in my ear: *Pay no attention to what is going on outside and around you. Do as I did. Listen for what comes through the inner doors and windows.*

I follow the instruction and focus on the inner sensorium. What enters is as much shape as sound, ideas that shift like iron filings on a magnetic field. The field becomes an ocean, the magnet, a star. Fish swim below or break the surface. Constellations dance in space without touching. I am back in last night's dream, beside the tall man in a black hoodie, whose face remains hidden. We are standing on the stern of the Pole Star watching a kingfisher dive.

Welcome to your dreamboat, whispers *Ferrini-Pedrolino*.

"How did I end up here?"

My question answers itself. Olson's poem "The Kingfishers," which shaped my vision as a young poet, has set up an inexorable connection to the obsession of my later years.

Olson never refers to Amfortas directly in the poem, but the message of my dream is the thread that connects "The Kingfishers" to the Fisher King. There is something to be learned by trolling the poem. I can't predict what will emerge but must see what lives in these waters.

Amfortas drops his line next to mine, and the orderly content of my inner world falls apart.

Pedrolino nods.

"Yes," I tell him. "I accept."

I'll take the risk, go where the currents lead. I am a navigator with faulty maps and a ragged compass. But there is a mystery waiting to be revealed, valuable clues to be drawn from the shadows into the light of day—if I am willing to make the journey.

Pedrolino is pleased. His smile deepens.

I tell him that following my public reading from *Fishing on the Pole Star*, I'd like to give a talk. The title just popped into my head, "Trolling with the Fisher King." That is, after all, where I find myself in the boat with Amfortas and Olson working the same lines, trolling for the same catch. I recall Yahweh's promise to Jeremiah after wounding Israel for their idolatrous bad behavior and sending his chosen ones into exile, "Who wounded thee, shall make thee whole." It is a chance to rekindle the psychological depth in myth as I did when I taught Mythology to students hungry for that connection.

I email my host, old Ferrini's nephew Henry, proposing the talk and its title, and suggest it immediately follow my reading.

Almost instantly I get a reply: "You're on!"

Pedrolino likes this.

Spreading the Net

There is room on my dream boat for those with unhealed wounds. My talk, "Trolling with the Fisher King," will bridge centuries. Parzival's mother, full of grief, stands at the rail, eyes closed, her line in the water. She shivers in a crimson shawl. I'm at a loss to address her.

"Say something," I tell the tall man.

There is no movement inside his hoodie. He pays out some line as he did when Parzival as the young knight stopped by the lake at dusk. In those days, Amfortas wore kingly robes which "could not have been richer if all the lands had been subject to him." Parzival took no notice of Amfortas' robes or peacock feathers when he addressed him and appeared indifferent to the clothes that marked changes in his own life. He traded those his mother made for a suit of armor, which he shed to don a robe of Arabian silk for the banquet at the Grail Castle. Parzival didn't recognize the consequences of his actions or the fate that awaited him. It might be argued that for the longest time Parzival didn't recognize himself. After the banquet, he woke to an empty castle and, back in his metal corset, rode out haunted by an inexplicable distress—what he recognized in the merciless silence of the moment was his *failure to recognize.*

The verb *to recognize,* and the failure to do so, drive Wolfram's narrative. It is through his failure to recognize his situation that Parzival becomes eventually aware of it. Today, this might be diagnosed as a "moral wound," as difficult to heal as the physical one that plagued Amfortas.

Recognition, Plato proposes in the *Meno,* is the act by which we remember what was known before and forgotten. When such a moment bursts into consciousness, it is often accompanied by a "shock." It may be the equivalent to an electric shock that rewires the brain; Nature's own ECT. I felt it on waking from my Fisher King dream after reading Olson's poem. It set me squarely on this ghost-skiff.

I've never knowingly begged a question or turned away from what asked to be recognized. Then why is it I feel the way I do now, as Parzival did when invisible voices jeered from the battlements?

"There must be a way to make sense of this."

It's your dreamboat, says *Pedrolino.*

Charles Olson smiles at me from a photograph on the wall. His expression is enigmatic but strangely reassuring, like a hand on my shoulder. I feel calmer about not knowing how I got here but resolve to follow in the wake of his poem "The Kingfishers." I will find a way to talk to the Fisher King, even though he will not talk to me.

ON THE TROLL

Mare Nostrum

My reading at the Gloucester Writers Center is scheduled for later this week. The poems in *Fishing on the Polestar* record my experience trolling the Bahamian outer islands for marlin, which we catch and release, as opposed to other native pelagic creatures like tuna, wahoo, and dolphin, which we catch and eat. The journey I describe includes exploring obscure inlets, uninhabited cays, remote lagoons and the crossing between Eleuthera and Columbus Point known as "the tongue of the ocean."

What would the tongue of the ocean say if it could speak?

In my Fisher King dream I'm using my childhood rig. Not the earliest one, a stick with a line and a hook, but a small fiberglass rod and spool reel. In those days I dug up night crawlers for bait in a section of Prospect Park where the earth was always damp. I later learned to handle a spinning reel, set the drag and cast and drop lures attached to a float. It was the middle rig I used in my dream, the one on which I hooked crappies (small sunfish) in Prospect Park Lake at the end of Harry S. Truman's second term.

Blues and stripers on party boats out of Sheepshead Bay, Montauk and Boston whalers in Long Island Sound saw me through the '60s. In the '70s, I took my kitchen staff at The Tin Palace fishing on weekends to provide dinner *specials* for the rest of the week.

In the '80s, I hauled snapper on a handline from a dugout off the coast of Belize.

Nothing was more exciting to me in the uncertain years at the end of the 20th century than crossing from Fort Lauderdale to the Bahamas in a 42-foot Bertram to troll for billfish. Starting from Bimini, we trolled as far south as Crooked Island and the Planas. One afternoon, boating an exquisitely iridescent female dolphin, I became aware of another dimension to this activity—the lure of what swam under the surface of my mind and in the deep drop darkness of my heart—and released the dolphin before her color faded.

I recognized what at some level I had known all along: fishing as metaphor. As a poet and psychotherapist drawn to the unconscious, I could set my lures to bring up the creatures concealed in my own depths. This also marked a new understanding of the Fisher King and why a line in the water brought relief. It guided me years later in my Mythology class, and there I thought to have laid it to rest—until I arrived in Gloucester and found myself on the troll again, fishing with a silent partner, who hides his face from me.

"The world is still wounded," I whisper. Pedrolino shakes his head.

"What?" I ask him.

"Prepare the baits," he says.

Preparing the Baits

Charles Olson's *Collected Works* lies on my bed open to his signature poem, "The Kingfishers."

Why not start here?

I read:

> *What does not change / is*
> *the will to change…*

And then, as though echoing my earlier state:

> *He woke, fully clothed, in his bed. He*
> *Remembered only one thing, the birds, how*
> *When he came in, he had gone around the rooms*
> *And got them back into their cage, the green one first,*
> *She with the bad leg, and then the blue,*
> *The one they had hoped was a male.*

Since the poem first appeared in 1949, no one has been able to give "The Kingfishers" a definitive reading. Some critics call the poem a dreamscape, and there is reason to treat it as such. Others cite it primarily as a response to post-Holocaust trauma. But what's most haunting about the poem is less historical than psychological. "The Kingfishers" occupies a limbic space between sleeping and waking. This is also where we locate the Grail Castle which appears and disappears—in a quantum dimension, beyond fixed coordinates.

Here, Olson drops his lures.

Lines from "The Kingfishers" float from dream-time into morning light trailing the brightly colored green and blue feathers of two caged birds. I hear seagulls squawk and cry outside over the marina, and the convenience store dumper on the other side of the parking lot. Seabirds have trailed in my wake for hundreds of miles.

As a merchant seaman, I crossed the Pacific with a swallow that hitched a ride from the Golden Gate in San Francisco to Subic Bay in the Philippines on our United Fruit reefer, the *Esparta*. Even through the roughest storms, when I thought such a creature could not have survived the gale, there it was the next morning perched on a boom. That swallow became my companion on the journey, a soul mate. Long after I returned from the South China Sea, the seabird haunts me. Like Olson's kingfishers, my *golondrina* exists as an ache in the present—an unhealed wound.

I follow my ghost bird into Olson's poem.

Neither "The Kingfishers" nor the Fisher King is primarily concerned with the act of fishing for its own sake; each links coherence to the function of fishing and fishing birds. Pursuit of coherence relieves the wound. Olson in this poem is fishing for clues. He has ingeniously prepared the bait: *what does not change/ is the will to change*. I will open my talk on the Fisher King with Olson's paradox.

Before I let out that spool, I examine the lure. What is attached to the line? It isn't "what doesn't change" that carries the charge, but the "will to change" and what that implies. We are drawn to what is concealed in *changeless will*. How can we take its measure? It is impervious to algorithms. Or the veiled operations of *gematria*, an esoteric system of numerical/verbal correspondences. *Changeless will* describes birth, death and renewal as a psychological, cosmological and quantum process, a grand design in its unfolding.

Mounting the Bounty, Wayne Atherton

I'll open my talk with Olson's caged green and blue kingfishers and the feathers they leave behind. The fact that they were caged from the start is significant. But first, I will invite Olson to come aboard the skiff. There's room for him, flanking Amfortas in his hoodie. The feathery remnants of Olson's poem, the seabirds, may be what we have to work with. We can use them as lures to draw down airborne companions of the way.

In my experience, birds track the baits.

I look for the *golondrina,* my ghost bird.

Fixing the Colors

I am 8 years old fishing in the park's brackish lake for crappies. My cork bobs on a bed of light that splinters where the float sinks abruptly. I raise the pole until what is on the end of my line breaks the surface. Sun splinters fly from my sunfish; *brightness falls from the air* (a line James Joyce borrowed from Thomas Nashe). The brilliance of its scales fires my imagination.

These sparks are evidence of an underwater rainbow. I want to pull it up whole. Everyone will marvel; it shines like no known thing, a jewel with rays that are endowed with superior powers, which will call forth the enormous power inside me. There is nothing beyond this, only the sensation of brilliance.

Disentangling the Net

At 16, deep-sea fishing with my father out of Miami, trolling our baits through the Gulf Stream, I sit in the fighting chair watching gulls and boobies swarm and dive, half aware that their patterns mirror those of fish below. My father, too, follows the seabirds with his sad eyes, until I get a hit on the line, and after what feels like a lifetime, I boat a small dolphinfish. She is stunning, with iridescent blue pectoral fins, the hues of blue and green on each side of her golden flanks. I immediately recognize the dolphin's life-changing colors as those I'd glimpsed in the Prospect Park sunfish and later on the tropical reefs at Key West and in Belize. They are all splinters of the same rainbow I had hoped to bring up whole as a child. Watching the dolphin's colors fade as she expires, it hits me full force. Having read Freud's *On Dreams* earlier that year, I understand that the rainbow I imagined exists only in the subterranean chamber of sleep. I make that connection between fishing in the Gulf Stream and trolling the unconscious on the stern of that charter boat, standing next to my father, my original wounded Fisher King. He joins the others on my ghost-boat.

Twenty years after my father's death, crossing the Tongue of the Ocean, I enshrine the unconscious as my primary fishing ground. Always mysterious, the trench between Nassau and Exuma reaches a depth of almost 7,000 feet at its southern end. Even more mysterious is the prospect of what I might find in my own depths, like the *barreleye* or *stoplight loosejaw* that ascend from the mesopelagic depths to feed at night closer to waking consciousness, or the bathypelagic *humpback anglerfish,* an ambush predator that attracts prey with a luminescent light, and the *red flabby whalefish* whose jaws fuse shut at maturity and from that point on lives on energy stored in its massive liver. The horrors and delights I have found there were, and remain, mesmerizing. I view them as I had the submerged rainbow, evidence of an intelligence buried in the psyche, that numinous jewel, the Grail.

Olson understood this as he prepared his lures. What was he fishing for? He quoted the 16th-century Belgian alchemist Gerhard Dorn, whose work Jung also found compelling psychologically: *"Color/ is the evidence of truth."*

Evidence came to light again in the blue and green of last night's dream from which I woke, like Olson's narrator, fully clothed. It follows me this morning like a seabird that breaks away, dives and comes up with something in its beak, and then is gone in a second. In my dream, I was again in the fighting chair, ready to reel in a marlin. I felt a tug, rocked back and forth like an orthodox Jew at prayer, until I had pulled up colors so bright they hurt my eyes. When my vision cleared, I was in a roomful of people dressed in green and blue, waiting to hear my talk. After bringing the dream to light, I'm blindsided by the image of such an audience, myself attempting to address a collection of brilliant feathers.

"This is not insignificant," I say to whomever may be listening, though I can't explain exactly why this is so.

Tracking the Ghost

Pedrolino responds as if reading my thoughts.
We trail lines defined by the color of our lures.
It's the way the lures ride that is important. They must imitate a motion that reads like a fish to other fish. Birds are not so easily fooled. I have never seen a seabird take the lure.

The first thing Olson does in "The Kingfishers" is to indicate that the green female bird "with the bad leg" and the blue male have been returned to their cage by someone named Fernand "who had talked lispingly of Albers & Angkor Vat" and subsequently leaves the party that is taking place.

> *When I saw him he was at the door, but it did not matter,*
> *he was already sliding along the wall of the night, losing himself*
> *in some crack of the ruins. That it should have been he*
> *who said, "The Kingfishers!*
> *who cares*
> *for their feathers*
> *now?"*

Fernand comments, then dissolves like a shadow in "some crack of the ruins." He points to what others at the party can't see, or seeing it, turn away. The shadow's voice, peripheral to awareness, delivers the message that draws us down, even as it hangs in the air like an accusation. The poet regrets that it should have been Fernand who poses the question: *Who cares?* The question had been his to ask. But like Parzival in the presence of Amfortas and the Grail, the part of Olson that might have asked the crucial question remains buried in his split-off shadow. He must become fully conscious to ask, *What ails thee?*

Fernand's question points to rather than discloses, the profound disconnection, and so rings as both desperate and ironic: *Who cares for their feathers now?*

Outraged, Olson raises a more pertinent question: Who is Fernand, this shadow that speaks unheard by any but the poet, then vanishes in a cloud of regret?

> His last words had been, "The pool is slime." Suddenly everyone,
> ceasing their talk, sat in a row around him, watched
> they did not so much hear, or pay attention, they wondered,
> looked at each other, smirked, but listened,
> he repeated and repeated, could not go beyond his thought
> "The pool the kingfisher's feathers were wealth why
> Did the export stop?"

"Who cares?" under these circumstances is a statement masquerading as a question. This party takes place around a pool, suggesting a mandalic center, a sacred space, however degraded, axial energies converging at that still point where time meets eternity.

Olson echoes Fernand's words. *The pool is slime.* Those confronted with a polluted center are unmoved.

The brightly plumaged birds at the opening of the poem were wounded and caged. At the end of the first section, the vestiges of their blues and greens, the feathers, have lost their value.

Value, as a quality, appears to be all but disappearing in a deteriorating natural world. The guests at this banquet, unlike those at the Grail Castle, remain indifferent, partying in a Wasteland.

Part one of "The Kingfishers" ends with the poet's observation: *It was then he left.*

Consciousness = The Wound

Aristotle observed: *To perceive is to suffer.*

Wolfram, who describes the impact of the Fisher King on those around him, would certainly agree. He might further have pointed out that suffering is more than a function of perception: Woundedness is inherent. One might equally reverse Aristotle's dictum and say: *To suffer is to perceive.* Both of these statements point to the risk/benefits of becoming conscious. On the one hand, it hurts. On the other, the conscious experience of pain is necessary for empathy, which is the precondition for transformation. Parzival at the banquet is too distracted by the spectacle to clearly see the suffering all around him. Instead of effecting a transformation, Parzival departs the following morning confused; he rides back into the Wasteland unchanged.

In a variation on this theme, Fernand's wakeup call is inaudible to those he addresses. After he slips away, the poet laments, "That it should have been he," as if the result might have been different had someone else, Olson himself, asked the question, maybe screamed it. Instead, question and questioner disappear unremembered except by the poet. As Olson renders it, suffering continues unperceived.

Mother Earth has always been wounded, but never before so unheard.

Her voice cries out in the earliest creation myths. Many of these, like the *Enuma Elish*, ("When on High") inscribed on seven clay tablets in the library at Ashur, describe the horrific violence that accompanies the movement from chaos to cosmos. Hero god Marduk confronts preconscious Chaos, a polymorphous feminine matrix in the form of a sea monster, Tiamat, and tears her in half to create earth and sky. In the Aztec creation, Quetzalcoatl, the morning star, and Tezcatlipoca, the night sky, become serpents to encircle crocodilian monster Cipactli, ripping into pieces to construct an orderly world which cries out for repayment in blood. "The Kingfishers" recalls both the wound embedded in creation and our failure to re-cognize it. The degradation of the psychological and natural worlds follow as surely as slime on the pool.

The Mysteries of dismembering and renewal are encoded in Neolithic sacraments, bread from yeast and beer from fermented grain. Egyptians in antiquity consumed Osiris wafers and beer to partake of an eternal blood and body. The Pyramid Text, dating to the 5th Dynasty (2,400 B.C.E.), instructs the king to rise from the tomb, transformed.

> Take your head, collect your bones,
> Gather your limbs, shake the earth from your flesh!
> Take your bread that rots not, your beer that sours not...

The once dismembered Osiris, is re/membered to become lord of the Underworld, with green skin, a pharaonic beard and ostrich feathers on either side of a canonical crown. The Fisher King wears a peacock feather in his. By their feathers you shall know them.

... feathers were wealth why / Did the export stop?"

Osiris, the Bronze Age bearer of woundedness, is another ghost on the Fisher King's boat.

We fish with feathers at the ends of our lines.

Spectral Navigation

Olson's question lingers: *Why/ did the export stop?*

He is referring to the kingfisher's feathers, vestiges of the sacred. They were valued not only as decorative, aesthetic objects, but as symbols of a transcendent function. We know the *why* of it. The feathers lost their value when no longer linked to the soul's journey, as they were by the Egyptians, where the scales of Ma'at are balanced by an ostrich feather.

When, in fact, did the export stop, the symbols cease to resonate?

In Bronze Age (ca.1600-1100 B.C.E.) Sumero-Akkadian myths like the *Enuma Elish*, the created world was the theater of the Gods.

Mortals were there to serve them, relieve their burdens, worship them and perform rituals of adoration. In Genesis, God tests mortals with punishments and rewards that often seem unreasonable but are suffered willingly, if not subject to negotiation. Pre-Socratic philosopher Protagoras declared, "Man is the measure of all things." By Wolfram's time, neutral angels have removed the Grail from the war in heaven and delivered it into the care of warring mortals—in what might as easily have been an act of desperation as of love. The sacred has over the centuries descended from the eternal order heaven to the ever-changing one we occupy on earth. And something has been lost in the process.

"What happened?" I challenge my companions.

Outside inside, inside outside, replies Pedrolino.

His meaning is clear: The sacred has been turned inside out, invisible to the material world, devalued like the kingfishers' feathers—which is not to say its archetypal power has ceased to exist. Evidence for the power of sacred symbols exists in the intelligence that shapes our dreams. While man may not be the measure of all things, he is the guardian of that measure.

Guarding the Measure

Wolfram describes Amfortas in his skiff, where Parzival first encounters him, as one "whose apparel could not have been richer if all lands had been subject to him. His hat was trimmed with peacock feathers." His royal plumes are linked to Lakshmi, Hera, Isis and Osiris, the Phoenix and the Bennu bird. Feathers emblazoned with the all-seeing eyes of Argus, on the peacock, sailed from India with the Phoenicians to Egypt and Syria, and to Jerusalem on King Solomon's fleet. (Kings 10:22, 2 Chron. 9:21). In Santeria, the peacock is sacred to Yemaya, Queen of the Seven Seas. The peacock feather establishes Amfortas' pedigree as a vestige of the sacred afloat on the surface of his watery world.

In Olson's poem "The Kingfishers," Fernand locates a vestige of the sacred in the pool become slime. The mandalic center has suffered through ignorance and neglect. This is not apparent to those at the party who sit around it. When Fernand tells them as much, they smirk for the same reason they fail to re/cognized kingfisher feathers as valuable. The Amfortas wound and the pool in need of repair both represent the potential for becoming conscious, to recognize and assign value.

Olson's focus on the slimy pool alludes to the process by which the Wasteland can be healed.

Wolfram evokes the same process in the course of resolving Amfortas' wound. In the opening phase of the Alchemical opus, decaying matter waits to be transformed into vital essence: the blackening, or *nigredo*. It is the first of four alchemical stages—the other three being the *albedo,* or whitening; *citrinitas*, the yellowing; *rubedo*, the reddening. Olson reinforces this connection by quoting the alchemist Gerhard Dorn: *Color is important.*

The blue and green kingfisher feathers have value. I caught as a child, sparks of the rainbow I imagined underwater and in the air as the indivisible embrace of the universe that held us all.

Olson and Wolfram understand that repair takes place by recognizing the wound as a vestige of the sacred. In "The Kingfishers" this is not articulated by the poet directly, but by Fernand, his wounded shadow. I suspect that it's not the *nigredo,* itself, that Amfortas and Olson fear, but that he (we/they) will get stuck in

> *a state between*
> *the origin and*
> *the end,*
> *between*
> *birth and the beginning*
> *of another fetid nest*

"What can we do?" I want to know.
Pedrolino answers, *Look for seabirds.*

SEABIRDS

Re/member Me

When Aeolus' daughter, Halcyon, attempts to follow her mortal husband, who has drowned in a storm, the wind god prevails on Zeus to turn the couple into birds. Zeus does this on the condition that Halcyon will nest for two weeks in mid-January ever year during which he will stay the waves and winds to let her young hatch in safety. This period becomes known as the Halcyon Days and the birds as kingfishers.

Olson emphasizes the kingfisher's ritualized behavior and comparison to the Phoenix or Egyptian Bennu bird, born from a nest of ashes. While popular legend relates that the Phoenix self-immolates in order to rise again from the ashes, another version holds that it simply decomposes and rises again from a bed of decaying matter.

Olson observes of the kingfisher:

> *It is true, it does nest with the opening year, but not on the*
> *waters. It nests at the end of a tunnel bored by itself in a bank.*
> *There,*
> *six or eight white and translucent eggs are laid, on fishbones not*
> *on bare clay, on bones thrown up in pellets by the birds.*

The kingfisher had long been on my list of unforgettable fishing birds, an impression that dates from 1982, when I explored the upper region of the Sibun River in Belize. I had set out by canoe with two companions on an uncharted stretch of river that flowed from the mountainous Pine Ridge to jungle lowlands. Birds were everywhere, anhinga, heron, hummingbird and toucan, all manner of parrot—but the activities of the riverine kingfishers were mesmerizing. They darted in and out of tunnels openings that formed fractal patterns in the muddy slopes on either side. Decomposed fish bone spilled out of these nests on to the river banks as we passed—visible and odoriferous, new life sprung from old life, *nigredo* to *rubedo*.

I have since spent untold hours on the troll watching birds circle or dive into weeds banked on shoals where small fish are feeding, larger ones under them and, at the bottom tier, great creatures with silver fins. Aloft on the tuna tower, a small seat perched on a 10-foot ladder rising from our bridge, I have admired the way seabirds weave together worlds above and below. Yet not as high or far below, for years the sun-drenched waters appeared to me to be as they'd always been. I was like one of those addressed by Fernand at the pool party, seduced by the surface, unaware of the slime.

Rising water temperatures in the southern Bahamas have become a breeding ground for stinging mites that make it impossible to swim without a wet-suit. Other changes, which had been in-cremental, can now be measured in bleached reefs, diminishing schools of tuna, the paucity of local catch and marlin moving farther south to Piñas Bay.

Sea birds—cormorant, frigate, pelican, heron and kingfisher—that dive with satellite precision are still there. They continue to connect the above to the below. What will become of them as the fish populations dwindle, whittled down by invasive species?

Cays with beaches that hold no footprint today serve as staged destinations. Bahamians from neighboring islands travel regularly to an otherwise uninhabited cay to set up a fake village for passengers on the Holland American Line. Tourists are deposited there for six hours to buy folk art, drink rum punch and dance to a reggae band. Six hours later they move on, unaware that this has been a virtual experience. At one time the beach might have hosted halcyon birds or the Pharaoh's imperishable swallows.

Before drifting off to sleep tonight in Gloucester, I am once again in the Bahamas, anchored in Concepcion Island's perfect teacup harbor at dusk, listening to Coltrane play "Ev'ry Time We Say Good-bye," until a skiff passes close enough for me to see the hooded figure trolling from its stern. It breaks my mood. I'm not safe from his haunt, even here. I call out to him, as if to prove that I will not be intimidated.

"There is slime in the pool!"

My voice trembles, but I think, or imagine, for an instant that the tall man in the hoodie glance in my direction.

Follow the seabirds! whispers Pedrolino.

"I do. I do."

I cleave to the *golondrina* who rode my United Fruit ship from the Golden Gate to the South China Sea through storms that seemed impossible for such a tiny creature to survive. I recognize something timeless in my swallow, its "changeless will."

That tiny figure continues to perch in my heart.

Focusing on Feathers

For centuries the swallow has been the sailor's talisman. Square-riggers were manned by seamen with barn swallows tattooed on their arms and chests. With good reason E.H. Gombrich tells us: "If you want to know where Egypt is, I suggest you ask a swallow." In autumn, swallows migrate over the Alps to the Nile Valley. In Dynastic Egypt it was commonly believed that the swallow could deliver a lost soul safely to the Underworld.

A Pharaoh tells us in the Pyramid Texts that he has "gone to the great island in the midst of the Field of Offerings on which the swallow gods alight; the swallows are the imperishable stars."

The Egyptian Underworld, the Duat, was not a subterranean world like the Greek Hades, with its entrance in a cave, but another dimension, that of the night sky, and lay deep within the Milky Way. In this sense, one might say, it was airborne, and most easily accessed by birds. But the drama of life, death and rebirth that takes place in the Duat at the behest of Osiris begins on earth by the Nile.

In the Ur-myth, Isis re/members the severed parts of her husband, Osiris, thrown into the Nile by his jealous brother, Seth. Ibis-headed Toth helps her to retrieve but the phallus, swallowed by a fish. This doesn't prevent Osiris from fathering an only begotten son, Horus, to be his representative on earth. Horus is identified with the Falcon.

Osiris presides over souls depicted as birds that fly into the underworld. The soul, dis/membered by death, is contained in the body of Osiris. Old Kingdom Pyramid Texts tell us that souls "regularly and continually" undergo a transformation in which the union of the *ba* (embodied soul) and the *ka* (vital spark) form a third, the *akh* (the effective one), the pure light of consciousness represented by a crested ibis, bird of Toth. Another Pyramid Text tells us that if the ferryman refuses to transport King Unas' soul to the other side, *He will leap and sit on the wing of Toth.*

Images of birds and feathers are everywhere on papyri and tomb walls.

Amon the "hidden source," or uncreated creator, is a feathered crow.

Amentet, the setting sun who prepares souls for rebirth appears with wings and holding a hawk's feather.

Shu, god of the atmosphere, wears ostrich feathers.

Isis sports a vulture headdress and the rainbow wings of a kite.

Osiris wears white ostrich feathers on either side of his crown.

Ra, the Sun and first Pharaoh, has a hawk's head.

Kephri at sunrise becomes the Bennu or risen Phoenix.

A single feather belonging to *Ma'at* on the scale in the Hall of Two Truths determines the fate of all souls. Souls lighter than her feather become *Akh* and are welcomed to paradise. Goddess of Balance, *Ma'at* spreads her ostrich wings over gods and humans.

The light of consciousness came to humankind through a line of perpetually wounded bearers starting with Prometheus and culminating with Amfortas. Olson's "Kingfishers" is a response to the dimming light, the vanished kingfishers that once lived on the Nile's banks are evidence of Mysteries that call unheard.

Their feathers are talismans.

The hieroglyph for feather (Shut) is an ostrich plume, sacred to Ma'at, whose tip bends under its own weight. An ostrich feather crowns Osiris in the Underworld. Amfortas wears a peacock feather, plumage sacred to Ra that evokes the radiance of the newly risen sun.

Swallows were identified in the Old Kingdom with the circumpolar stars that did not set, a quality that made them perfect vehicles for souls in the afterlife. As the Pyramid Text tells us: *the swallows are those who do not set–and they will give this [Pharaoh] Pepi that wood of life which they live on.*

Isis assumed the shape of a swallow to fly around the pillar enclosing Osiris' coffin before bringing him back to life. Intuited from the first but unrealized until this moment, the impact of a certain swallow on a young seaman watching a storm from the stern of the *Esparta*: that *golondrina* was, and remains, my *ba-bird*.

FIXING THE COLOR

He thought of the E on the stone, and of what Mao
said la lumiere
> *but the kingfisher*
de l'aurore
> *but the kingfisher flew west*
est devant nous!
>> *he got the color of his breast*
>> *from the heat of the setting sun!*

The Rubedo, The Reddening

Olson opens Section 2 of "The Kingfishers" with the observation: *but the kingfisher flew west,* where Ancient Egypt located the entrance to the under-world and the beginning of the Sun's Night Sea Journey. The setting sun, Horakhty, was thought to die when he dipped below the horizon. At the

Ra on the sun barque with the Bennu Bird, 1200 B.C.E.

entrance to the Underworld he sets out in his boat to sail by night through the world of the dead. These are dark waters where he risks total extinction to unite with Osiris and be reborn as the scarab beetle, Khepri, the newly risen sun. Jung suggests that "The purpose of nearly all rebirth rites is to unite the above with the below," the conscious with the unconscious.

Olson's avian avatar, the kingfisher, flies west, redness baked into its breast by the setting sun. Like my *golondrina*, he is one of the birds on Ra's night boat, *Mesektet.* The seabirds are allies. They will sail with Ra through 12 houses corresponding to the hours between sunset and sunrise, each with its own dangers.

A Coffin Papyrus depicts three *ba-birds* in the fifth hour, there to protect Ra against Chaos, the serpent *Apophis*. Ra grows darker and weaker as the hours pass; even his guardians are afraid. There is no guarantee that chaos will not swallow Ra's light. According to some, he actually dies. At the darkest hour, in the deepest part of the underworld, just when it seems that all may be lost, Osiris, "the Hidden Soul," meets Ra face to face. In that moment the high-voltage transformation takes place: the Two become One by forming a Third, the enlightened *akh*.

Gerhard Dorn, in his alchemical treatise, speaks of a "hidden third" as "the medium enduring until now in all things." Jung refers to this as the *Transcendent Function,* the resolution born from the tension between opposites. Khepri rises like a fire in the east. It is the last stage of the transformation alchemists call the *rubedo,* the reddening. The seabird bears witness, and at the end of the day it is the kingfisher who begins again to ride the boat into the night sea, the red baked into its breast.

On a cosmic level, this happens nightly.

Both Ra's Night Sea Journey and that of Amfortas fishing from his skiff on Lake Brumbane highlight the importance of the wound as an agent of transformation: The rebirth of light is effected in the dark through suffering. In the words of a Hymn to Osiris: "Thou risest in the horizon, thou givest light through the darkness."

Seabirds will follow a ship across the ocean or descend on the gunnels into the Underworld.

I've learned to look for them. Especially where the seas are uncharted and there is the risk of being devoured by the dragon called Chaos. The Egyptians believed that the fate of world depended on this journey of risk and transformation. It becomes the template for the soul after death, and also for the wounded savior figures to follow. Among these I number my shipmate Amfortas.

Shades of Red

In contrast to Ra's journey of renewal, Olson invokes the self-mythologizing post-industrial Pharaoh, Mao, who said, "History is a symptom of our disease," and forbade traditional customs like binding women's feet, Confucian protocols and the 4,000-year-old practice of consulting the oracle. Mao's sun defied the notion of a Night Sea. The sun of his Cultural Revolution (1966-76) never set, and at the same time it attempted to obliterate any memory of Eastern spiritual traditions. Lu Dongbin's seventh-century Taoist treatise on "inner" alchemy, *The Secret of the Golden Flower,* survived the purge because it was translated into German by Richard Wilhelm (1929), with an introduction by Carl Jung.

Mao replaced the mysteries of risk and transformation with historical revisionism. Its rites of Social Engineering denied the existence of the historical unconscious. Mao flew, as Olson notes, in the opposite direction to the kingfisher. In 1949, as leader of the People's Republic of China, Mao outlined his revolution in a *Report to the Second Plenary Session*:

"We are not only good at destroying the Old World, we are also good at building the new." Mao's vision, codified in his *Little Red Book*, flew in the opposite direction of Jung's monumental *Red Book* (1916-23), which locates the historical unconscious as a layer under the personal one and encourages dialogue with the ancestors.

Mao wasn't interested in alchemy, inner or outer. The ancestors that gave meaning to Confucian society became anathema in his regime. Commerce with the dead, listening for their messages, constituted a capital offense. The doctrine of Historical Irrelevance stoked the bonfire of revolution which then prohibited the creation of a "past." Mao's advocacy of continual revolution took Olson's observation, "the only thing that doesn't change is the will to change" and turned it inside out. Mao's *la lumiere* reduced time and change to a political process that unfolds under a sun that never sets.

While I consider this, I notice that Olson's evocation of Mao has created an unmistakable restlessness on our skiff where the ghosts of wounded light-bearers hold their lines. No doubt we are operating in the slipstream of seabirds that have become scarce, their feathers a hedge against soul loss. I pose two silent questions to my shipmates, invite whomever to step up and answer one or both of them.

What happens if we are unable, even in a meager way, to bring Osirian intelligence to light?

And what has Mao got to do with this?

Certainly, Olson feared that our loss of the Mysteries might be beyond repair. But more to the point, in the irony of unintended consequences, it's possible that what Mao attempted to do in China by coercion we are accomplishing now by attrition.

Trolling with the Fisher King

The Alchemical Nest

What will you tell them? asks Pedrolino.

He is referring to the audience dressed in green and blue who have come to hear my talk on "Trolling with the Fisher King."

"What can I say? The situation looks bad."

But you started off with such hope.

I shrug.

If they were sitting in front of me now, I'd say, "Chaos stalks our high-tech lives. A smart hacker-child can send the systems that enable civilization into a tailspin. Our personal infrastructures remain largely unattended. The Underworld is no longer the place in which souls are weighed or Ma'at restores balance with a feather. Our psychology is haunted by forces denied, degraded or disguised as ideologies, religious and political, that set us at odds. Our projections are fueled by *Thanatos*, an unconscious death wish. The ecology deteriorates while gods past and present disappear beneath the waves."

Will you leave it there?

Pedrolino's question is rhetorical.

This black figure in his domed hat outlined by a white line on a black field gazes down from his post on the wall. His moon face glows like polished silver. I stare into the soul of old Ferrini, author of *Know Fish*.

"Shall I tell those who come to hear my talk that every time I address Amfortas, he turns away?"

Talk about the troll.

His words run through my mind. When only feathers are left, we must use them as lures. A shaman can use a single bone to re/constitute the entire body.

> *...it does nest with the opening year but not on the waters.*
> *It nests at the end of a tunnel bored by itself in a bank.*
> *There Six or eight white or translucent eggs are laid, on*
> *fishbones Not on bare clay, on bones thrown up in pellets*

"I'll describe the Sibun River, the nests on its banks."

Keep trolling.

I can smell the rotting fish bone chips from my canoe. Eggs warmed by the heat of that decaying nest will hatch on the bones of their prey. It suddenly strikes me that Olson constructs his poem in the way kingfishers build their nests, with the remains of rotting fish bones. He gathers all the "rejectamenta," the decaying splinters of myth, as well as personal and historical memory. From its heat, words are born, take flight, hover, and dive.

Pay attention, whispers Pedrolino. *"You're close."*

I stop and listen. An idea enters through an open inner window—an insight. Not simply a piece of information, but an epiphany. I must get my audience to bring all the senses to bear—to hear the birds chatter, feel the river flow beneath the craft, touch the oars, the gunnels, smell the decaying bone chips, let the sulphurous odor of the nests sting their nostrils.

I can hatch my talk from the decaying nest.

I'll ask my audience to imagine the heat of infected flesh and the sandalwood of hope in the presence of such wounds, telling them that Olson has redefined my feelings about being on the skiff with Amfortas, and my father, and all the other ghosts that appear at the rail. I still believe Olson has the key. Instead of answering the questions he raises in the opening of "The Kingfishers," he shifts the emphasis from product to process. What happened to the kingfishers is never answered *in* the poem—but *by* the poem, a nest of bones to hatch a seabird. What fledges from it dives like a kingfisher into my unconscious.

Re-viewing

"The Kingfishers" begins with a comment that might easily go unremarked: *He woke, fully clothed, in his bed. He / remembered only one thing, the birds...*

I might've disregarded it entirely had it not been for the spirit of place that spoke to me, as he does now on the day of my poetry reading, followed by a discussion of the Fisher King.

What brought you here?

I'm trying to determine why I proposed a lecture that I now feel unable to deliver. At first I'm tempted to say "the birds." Perhaps, like Fernand, it was their feathers that moved me. I've had the same dream over the last few nights. *I'm in a room full of folding chairs. They are empty at first, then people file in to fill them. They've come to hear my talk. I smile at them. They smile back. Everyone is dressed in blue and green. I wake in cold sweat.*

"I need time to tie things together."

You have five hours.

It suddenly dawns on me that I am fishing for a way to understand woundedness as an ongoing condition, pain as perception, a guide to reuniting the split-off parts of the soul, the ba and the ka, to form a third, the akh (the effective one). But I'm not sure how to discuss what has become of this process. The line of fishermen as wounded light-bearers no longer compels recognition.

Listen, counsels Pedrolino.

I wait for him to complete his thought, then realize that this word is a command, not a request. I'll tell my audience in folding chairs that they must keep their lines in the water, look for sea birds, and listen for what Olson calls the voice, *"heard differently//as in another time,"* that comes through us but supersedes our own.

"So much depends on it."

Ahhh, he sighs.

CHECKING THE LINES

In his Holocaust memoir, *Night*, Elie Wiesel describes the secret teaching received by his young alter-ego, Elie, before the entire *shtetle* was transported to Auschwitz. Bare-foot Moshe the Beadle, who cleans the synagogue, instructs his young protégée, "At the end of your life God measures you by the depth of your question."

In this teaching, the question answers itself by deepening. What lies too deep for words is seeded in the wound. Here, the pain embedded in the created world—Osiris dismembered and the Fisher King unhealed are caught in what Olson calls "the net of being" and begs us, with their help, to disentangle it.

Wiesel listened in silence to those ghosts from the moment he walked away from Auschwitz until his death in 2016. They instructed him. The wound must be re/membered. It compels the question to deepen. Such is the wisdom he imparted in *Night*, which portrays unfathomable human depravity under the veneer of civilization, capable of destroying cultures and turning cities into rubble.

Olson formulates it in another way:

> *I pose you your question:*
> *Shall you uncover honey / where maggots are?*
> *I hunt among the stones*

The question comes in many forms, but the depth is plumbed where Ra meets Osiris, in the fifth house of the Night Sea Journey, as the seabirds look on.

Olson asks, *"The Kingfishers! / Who cares/ For their feathers/ Now?"*

Holden Caulfield, in *Catcher in The Rye*, wants to know, *"Where do ducks in winter go?"* Chretien de Troyes' *Perceval* eventually inquires, *"Whom does the Grail serve?"*

Von Eschenbach's Parzival whispers, *"What ails thee?"*

But what if the question itself is forgotten, lost, out of reach—or, more to the point, there is no one to bring it full-voice into the world?

We then must listen for our ghosts, ask them to talk to us, like Odysseus at the edge of Erebus hoping to find his way home. They are the enduring connection to what has passed beyond our grasp. As Olson tells us: *they are the dead in ourselves, / I cry out to you, / disentangle the nets of being!* They can confirm or deny the operations in the underworld to unify the soul's split-off parts, the *ka* and *ba* of us, into the *akh*, or pure light of consciousness. At stake is our ability to deepen the question.

Sometimes on my ghost boat, when I call out to Osiris, Olson raises his head from the lines and stares at me before returning to the baits.

C.G. Jung captures the Fisher King Function in *Memories, Dreams, Reflections*: "One does not become enlightened by imagining figures of light, but by making the darkness conscious."

When Jung spoke at Harvard in 1938, Olson sought him out and engaged him in conversation about Herman Melville. There is no darker figure than Melville's wounded seagoing Captain Ahab, who pursues the white whale to the brink of the abyss. After finishing *Moby Dick,* Melville commented in a letter dated 1851 to Nathaniel Hawthorne, "I have written a wicked book, and feel spotless as the lamb." And later in the same letter, "I feel that the Godhead is broken up like the bread at the Supper, and that we are the pieces."

Two years after Olson met Jung at Harvard, Jung's *Psychology and Alchemy* explored the importance of symbols fished up from the collective unconscious. Olson's "The Kingfishers" appeared in 1949, four years after the liberation of Auschwitz and the bombing of Hiroshima redefined civilization. Those who bring such consciousness to light must suffer a Promethean wound. It's a condition of the gift.

Disentangling the Net

This afternoon I walk through town to Fort Street to find the modest multiple-dwelling house looking out at the channel leading into Gloucester Harbor. A plaque affixed to the peeling white wall is the only evidence that Olson lived there. It is also a tribute to the insistence of Henry Ferrini, Vincent's nephew and my host at the Gloucester Writers Center, who petitioned the city fathers for the installation until they relented. Today, Gorton's huge plant, which hugs the shore along Rogers Street facing the State Fish Pier, processes frozen catch from foreign waters. The depleted local fishing grounds, and the plant that packages fish for export, echo the missing kingfishers in the poem. I recall that it was Olson who coined the term that defined such an age, post-modern. And that he found in Gloucester material to create a monument to intimations of the sacred as it slips away.

THE ARCHAEOLOGY
OF DREAMS

Seth Butler, Crossing the River Styx

See how slow and
sure I glide. See my organs
*   wings. And you, little*

fish I once plunged for
–nameless invisible fish in deepest darkest ocean.

Changing, Richard Berengarten

BREAKFAST AT NICK'S

Bran Muffin Blues

For several years after returning from Vietnam to the bewildering streets of New York's Lower East Side, I spent hours every morning at Nick's Diner on the corner of Second Avenue and Fourth Street recording dreams. The images that I brought back nightly from sleep, embedded in dramas that pointed to meanings I could almost, but not quite, understand were irresistible and relentless. The Greek proprietor in his lightly stained white apron and with a half-smoked cigarette, the pale blue eyes peeking out of thick, black rimmed glasses, was a guardian at the gate. At Nick's, I could sink into my dream-world and feel safe. I would later think of the diner as a temple like one of those dedicated to the Greek god of healing, Asclepius. As early as the fourth century B.C.E., pilgrims came to spend the night in one of the secret chambers "incubating" dreams or visions for a priest to interpret and then prescribe the appropriate therapy. At Nick's, my own Asclepieion, I followed the procession of dream images to their destination as the smell of coffee, home fries and bacon wafted from the grill.

Now and then I'd find the diner closed and knew the proprietor had gone to the racetrack.

Otherwise, I could depend on the white-haired man leaning on the counter to nod as I entered. There were seldom more than five or six customers, mostly on the stools, perhaps one or two at a table. But not my table, a two-seater at the window with a view of Café La Mama across the street. One of the regulars at the counter, a man who made random duck noises, bothered no one. In minutes, Nick set my toasted bran muffin and mug of coffee down next to my open notebook. He did it soundlessly, then returned to his post.

I ate slowly, seated next to the one evidence of nature in the room, a drooping potted snake plant, and began to write what I recalled. When I began this exploration, I felt lucky to remember one or two dream fragments. Slowly, my ability grew stronger, and I retained whole dreams and dream sequences until I found myself spending as much as three hours every morning at the task. More time than I'd thought possible.

Once the dreams were recorded, I floated through, no, over them like a man on a glass-bottom boat above a coral reef. Their colors danced just below a transparent surface, shapes shifting slightly depending on the current. All kinds of aquatic life showed up to feed. I let out my lines and watched, never feeling rushed.

Nick seemed to understand that I was fishing for something important in much the same way he handicapped the Daily Racing Form. We did it together. With a minimal exchange of words we shared a a growing sense of the fact that we were similarly compelled.

It went on like this for three years, until a stand of bleacher seats at Aqueduct fell on Nick.

The diner disappeared and almost instantly, as in a dream, it became a bodega.

What started at Nick's has shaped my process as a poet, and later my practice as a psychotherapist. In the privacy of my office I've worked with clients' dreams as I do my own, trolling for images that might give shape to patterns that drive their lives unseen.

In this respect, too, I think of myself as part of a lineage dating back to Asclepius, in whose temples people engaged their dreams. One version of the myth tells us that when Asclepius' powers became so powerful that he could bring souls back from the dead, Zeus killed him with a thunderbolt that reverberated like the collapsing stands at Aqueduct. Not surprisingly, I picture the gentle physician in a white apron behind a Formica counter reading the Racing Form.

Before Socrates died of self-administered hemlock, he asked his faithful friend Phaedo to remember to bring Asclepius a cock in payment for an old debt. I can easily believe that in his search for truth Socrates recognized in his own dream work with Asclepius an alternative to his own dialectic, one that confronted the unconscious in the temple dream chambers. And the manner of payment, a cock, represented this as a wakeup call.

Nick's diner was my "dream incubator." And I'm convinced that there are inescapable correspondences between Nick and Asclepius.

Both Greeks died violently, Asclepius from a thunderbolt hurled by Zeus as punishment for bringing shades back from the dead and Nick, under falling bleachers at Aqueduct while calculating the odds on the Trifecta. Socrates, as we know, died by his own hand in his own time, refusing the opportunity Phaedo offered him to escape a death sentence imposed on him for corrupting the youth of Athens. Whatever Socrates had uncovered in this pursuit left him unafraid to cross the threshold. In this respect, too, I believe Nick was also Socratic. I'd like to think that in the eternal instant that preceded death as the bleachers fell on him, Nick managed a smile.

Years after Nick's diner had disappeared like the spectral Grail Castle, I would realize that Parzival's journey was my own. Long before I knew the names of Parzival or Amfortas, I intuited the shape of their connection. I'd glimpsed the Intelligence that composed their journey over coffee and bran muffins. When I met them several years later through Wolfram, it seemed that I'd known them all my life. This glimpse in anticipation of what is yet to come is part of the legacy I take with me from Nick's. It continues to inform my work today as a practicing psychotherapist, and to connect those who do this work to the physicians who helped bring dreams to light in the fourth century B.C.E., and were known as "Therapeutae," therapists of Asclepius.

OPHIUCHUS

Strange Bait

In February 1966, at the age of 26, I disembarked from the S.S. Esparta at Seattle-Tacoma after six months in Vietnam. The journey took me from a war-ravaged land to one torn by civil strife. I'd watched homeless orphans in Saigon sell mariposas to GIs, while counterculture children in Haight-Ashbury got high and pinned flowers in their hair. Timothy Leary instructed his audiences to "turn on, tune in and drop out," as Henry Kissinger advocated carpet bombing and the use of Agent

Orange. Protesters chanted to end the war and vilified soldiers who brought the abyss back with them.

Saturn devoured his children on both ends of this continuum.

The cultural nightmare also laid waste to any claim to sanity by those in authority, let alone to the balance and trust required for healing. The fantasy that leadership could still be moral lay like discarded film footage on the cutting-room floor as we filled that vacuum with a technology that can spin any condition into its opposite. Now, hyper stimulation and desensitization walk hand in hand. Pain hardens into confusion or explodes in acts of terror. Disconnection and deception loom at every intersection of the Information Superhighway just as environmental degradation dances cheek-to-cheek with urban gentrification. My glimpse into Parzival's world anticipated this, where knights like Amfortas left a trail of heartbreak to do battle in the name of love. *Parzival* may be the first tale on record to identify the evolving wound in Western culture as a failure of intimacy.

At the current rate of change, what transpired in a century now happens in a decade. We are on a rocket ship, pressed by the G-force and fortified against it by all manner of prosthetic devices. But the basic structure of the human psyche has not changed since our ancestors inscribed their images swimming in the Paleolithic darkness of those great caves. I have no idea how to approach the problems that arise from this condition on a massive scale. As a therapist, I do the best I can addressing one person at a time.

Wolfram's work speaks to what I see around me even though it was composed eight centuries ago. The figures in his narrative wear armor, fight with swords and swear allegiance to hierarchical authorities. The equivalent of these figures and their protocols in our own time are shadows on the periphery. What shapes do those shadows take today, and how are they embedded in the particulars of our lives?

A CASE HISTORY

My client Perry could be Parzival, or cut as closely from that physical cloth as anyone who meets him might imagine. At 6-foot-2, he has linebacker shoulders. His blue eyes, set under a broad brow, give him the look of an eagle focused on a world of prey. A leonine mane of blond hair heightens the impression of a warrior, balanced by a dentally blessed open smile. Heads turn when Perry enters a room. A survey of his gifts reveals that he is a discerning collector of folk art, stalwart conservationist and outdoorsman, formidable chef and sommelier and a canny businessman. In the course of 50 years, Perry has made a living as a rock drummer, nightclub owner, music producer and currently as a high-end realtor. His version of the Grail mission is to be the best possible human being he can, which includes helping those he cares for in any way he can. Admittedly, it is also shaped by his ambition to win the admiration and gratitude of those around him. Perry projects the image of the fantasy lover. Women are drawn to him as they might be to a knight who will slay the dragons of loneliness, disappointment and a history of trauma. In spite of his charm, the issue that troubles him most is his inability to sustain romantic relationships.

Parzival's confusion upon leaving the Grail Castle could also describe what Perry feels after the loss of intimacy. His relationships, mostly well-intentioned, turn out to be fragmented and ambivalent. Following the initial exhilaration of a new alliance, Perry often feels trapped and has to flee. On occasion, the intensity of his pursuit drives the object of his affection away. This pattern is the source of great pain and self-doubt. Perry struggles to understand why the condition exists and what he might do about it.

His situation reminds me of Shakespeare's Sonnet #31:

> Thou art the grave where buried love doth live,
> Hung with the trophies of … lovers gone…

Our sessions over five years have focused on the wounds inflicted by Perry's sadistic father and enabled by his narcissistic mother.

Physical and emotional violence suffuse his earliest memories. He compartmentalizes the circumstances in his childhood that produced unrelieved terror, along with pervasive feelings of anger, shame and worthlessness. As he grew older, when things heated up at home Perry retreated to his room, the cave where he beat out rhythms with drum sticks on a practice pad and imagined himself a rock star in a silver jumpsuit.

When we first met, Perry exuded a strong *bonhomie*. The traumatic events of his youth appeared to have given way in his adult life to strong friendships, fine wines and gourmet meals balanced by regular workouts at the gym. Only Perry's repeated failures in relationships with women raised the alarm. He drifted in a wake of botched intimacies, questioning why his desire to love and be loved became claustrophobic and life-threatening. Perry claimed that he was not trapped by the idea of domesticity, but rather his fear of it. Rooted in his early traumas, the prospect of a durable attachment set off his instinctive response to life- threatening danger: flight.

Until he met Cassandra.

There was something about Cassie that would not let him go. From the first, he held onto her even when she pushed him away. She expressed doubts about her ability to satisfy his needs. His life was already filled with people who shared his enthusiasms for folk art, music and banquet-style gourmet meals with the right wine. Social occasions made her uncomfortable. Perry insisted that his friends would not threaten their closeness. For the first time in recent memory, he felt no desire to run. He continued to find her Nordic good looks irresistible. Six months into the relationship, they'd moved from casual content to talk of commitment.

Cassie balked.

Perry insisted they take it slowly. He wanted to be careful, reassuring her that he understood what it felt like to be overwhelmed. For once it was possible for Perry to maintain something different than in past experiences.

Over the following months, it became clear that Cassie's unhealed wounds were in many ways similar to his. Repeated sexual abuse by her stepfather, denied until this day by her mother, had not affected her ability to function at a high level in daily life. She was impeccably groomed, consistent with her duties as an office manager. After business hours she preferred to avoid unfamiliar social situations. Cassie was happy to lounge around in sweats on weekends with her three cats.

Naturally social, Perry tried to accommodate her without giving up what he felt important for his own well-being. Cassie complained when he spent time hunting and fishing alone or socializing with friends. Perry invited her to work on their issues in couples' therapy. Cassie agreed initially, appeared for several sessions, but then declined to continue.

The situation remained tense.

At our next weekly session, Perry appeared unusually upset. He had caught Cassie going through his emails and cell phone records. She responded to his protests by questioning him about his contacts. He tried to quiet her suspicions about his communications with other women, mostly in the course of doing business in real estate. Perry could say little to defend himself from her charges. His attempts to explain his relationships read to her like alibis. She couldn't pin it down but was certain he'd been unfaithful.

"There's no way to reason with her," he told me.

Perry made it clear that he couldn't continue with her under these conditions. He was unable to fix what was broken in Cassie. After almost a year, an unprecedented period of time for him in a relationship, Cassie was forcing him out.

He sat facing me, full of grief. I tried to comfort him, complimented his work in therapy on this relationship, regardless of the way it might end.

"It's ground gained," I offered.

"What ground?"

In drawing close to Cassie, I told him, he'd had more than a glimpse of what it felt like to be loving and unafraid. While it didn't relieve his grief in the moment, this was a concrete experience of the possibilities that awaited him in the future, of who he might become in relationship to another, and it moved him.

What We Fish For

In search of a night's lodging, Parzival followed the directions given by a man he encountered fishing. He found the Grail Castle at dusk. Later, at the banquet in the Great Hall, he was struck by the abundance of the table at which he was seated but had only a limited awareness of anything else. He registered Amfortas' deepening furrows and compressed lips but had been taught that a knight didn't question his host. Until Parzival felt the weight of his own grief, he would remain buried in false assumptions and burdened by failure.

The comparison wasn't lost on Perry. After hearing the story for the first time, he went home and ordered a copy of *Parzival*. He read it, even as he felt himself to be living so much of it. I made the point that it was not unusual to find ourselves dumbfounded at life's banquet. A few of us glimpse in advance the image of our unique destiny. Though it may not be fully recognizable as such, it propels us into the field from which it arises. This glimpse, however it comes to us, activates our feeling and intuition, along with the drive to grasp what waits to be named before we can name it.

The Glimpse

Parzival had a glimpse of eternity in time shortly after he first arrived at the Grail Castle. On his way to the banquet hall, he paused in front of a small room on his left. A grey-bearded elder, "greyer than even mist," lying on a bed inside the room, lifted his head to meet the young knight's eye. Parzival felt something inside of him stir. The old man appeared to float on a bed of light. Suddenly, Parzival's heart was filled with tenderness, an emotion he had not encountered before. He wanted to find out more about this old man but learned only that his name was Titurel before his attendants urged him on to the Great Hall, the scene of what would be his epic failure.

We know what happened after that: He woke to an empty castle. His horse waited, but there were no other horses in the stalls. Though the castle appeared empty, voices followed him as he rode out. The drawbridge closed behind him. Jeers from the battlements accused him of lacking a heart as well as a tongue.

What followed was confusion.

The nature of his offense eluded him until, after riding for several hours, he encountered a woman keening over a dead knight. She revealed herself to be his cousin Sigune. The corpse she refused to let go of was her lover, who died in defense of Parzival's kingdom during his absence. She made the depth of his failure clear. This corpse was one of many who died for his sake.

Parzival was struck dumb. What he imagined to be his legacy of noble deeds was, in fact, a list of failure upon failure.

Parzival failed because he was unconscious. What he'd assumed was his mission had been a vague thing, a series of acts he'd ascribed to his inherent knightly virtue. He had yet to learn the whole truth about himself. He rode away, leaving Sigune with her lover's corpse and the Wasteland unchanged. What he took away with him was something he'd experienced on his way to the banquet hall the night before. It was linked in his memory to the beautiful old man he'd glimpsed floating on a bed of light. The glimpse had connected him, in a way he could not have understood in that moment, to the original Grail King, his great-uncle, Titurel.

The importance of this glimpse must be noted; it's a significant developmental milestone. Such a glimpse activates the process of becoming conscious. It will take Parzival 20 years of wandering, struggle and disappointment before he realizes that what he glimpsed in that moment was his destiny.

What else did Parzival register in the figure of Titurel through a crack in the door?

"The Wounded Fisher King"

Perhaps the wise ancestor who has known the end from the beginning, and therefore glimpse himself, redeemed: the Grail Keeper buried like a genetic memory in his own unconscious.

Perry, also, might've glimpsed his possible redemption in Cassie's loving gaze, the promise of something he had never experienced before. Perry and Parzival both felt rather than understood the depth of such connection. Neither could have explained it. Perhaps all fishermen are drawn to that split-off part they imagine flashing under the surface that makes one whole—Osiris' phallus swallowed by a fish.

ENTER THE FISHERMAN

Reading the Water

Perry is a lifelong fisherman. He is at his best on the bank of a trout stream casting out line. The years have taught him to read the water for patterns, flow, and bottom. Perry chooses his lures carefully and knows where and how to place each one. In session he talks about his dreams in the language of fishing because it makes the references easier to understand.

Dreams and lucid visions hit Perry's line regularly.

The catch can be playful or smart, or if he is not attentive, it can easily snag and break the monofilament. He is, however, quick to tell me that fishing for dreams differs significantly from what he does at a trout stream in one respect. Fishing for dream content, he is at times repelled, and at others fascinated by what he reels in. But certain things hold true for both.

"I don't always catch something or keep what I catch."

I ask him if he ever throws the most remarkable images back. Perry smiles.

Fishing for trout holds none of the dangers inherent in fishing for his dreams. The sense of utter vulnerability is absent when he is standing in the stream, knee-deep in waders. He loves getting lost in the senses, watching light and shadow shift along the banks, hearing the current murmur, feeling a breeze touch his cheek. The variables there are inviting rather than confusing. Some of his best days are those when he doesn't get a bite.

This may be true for the Fisher King as well. In that silence, when the baits are still, one reads the water as if there were no message between the lines. Just the lines themselves, hypnotic, moving as they should on the troll. Amfortas, like Perry, may well find the rhythms in real time predictable and soothing. The problem for Perry arises when fishing in psychological space/time, where the depths rise up. Even the nibble of a creature in the deep psyche, imprinted with the numinous, can be disturbing.

"Can you pull in Leviathan with a fish hook or tie down its tongue with a rope?" asks God in Job 41.

When Perry runs into something too heavy for his psychological hook, he takes a break from therapy. And with good reason. Most spiritual traditions warn against just such a situation. In the Jewish tradition, Merkabah mystics are warned never to gaze directly at the Throne, lest they be reduced instantly to a cinder. Only a divinely ordained but clinically mad Ezekiel or Moses on the mount can risk drawing close to the ineffable. God warns Job directly not to stare too deeply lest he provoke the Leviathan:

His snorting throws out flashes of light; his eyes are like the rays of dawn. Firebrands stream from his mouth; sparks of fire shoot out. Smoke pours from his nostrils as from a boiling pot over a fire of reeds.

The Fisherman's Lament

"I feel empty," Perry opens our session. "Nothing seems to last. Nothing of value." I hear Parzival suddenly aware he exists in a Wasteland.

In Perry's case, the Wasteland is a professional workshop he participated in along with other real estate brokers who deal in multimillion-dollar properties facilitated by a noted motivational speaker. After recognizing them as a lively group of high achievers, she challenged them to close their eyes and picture what success looked like to each of them. More specifically, she wanted to know how they saw themselves at the height of their success and what they would choose to do with their money. It was meant to be a goal-orienting exercise, a glimpse of their destination, the longed-for reward each was working so hard to realize.

"I started to cry." Perry flushed.

"Why?"

For him this invitation did not call forth grandiose images. Instead, Perry found himself staring into the abyss. He would not tell me what he saw, himself as a child watching as his father shot his dog to make a point or his father as a demented old man incapable of apology or blessing—but it brought tears to his eyes.

"Unbecoming in a man after 45."

"What do you make of it?

"I don't know." He rubs his chin, Perry's anxiety tell. "They keep urging us to reject pain and embrace pleasure. But for some reason, I'm always moving in the opposite direction."

I repeat Victor Frankel's contention that the dream of material wealth fills the void left by the absence of meaning. Perry has read *Man's Search for Meaning* and agrees. Still, it is hard for him to let go of the material dream. On the other hand, after so much time pursuing it, material success feels meaningless to him. Surrounded by those at the workshop, all of whom were driven by the desire for wealth, he became nauseous.

"Maybe that's a good thing," I offer.

"Easy for you to say."

Perry's attempt to fill his emptiness with intimacy had produced the same reaction. His breakup with Cassie filled him with regret and left him at times nauseated. He had been determined not to follow his past pattern and had held firm until the weight of her accusations had proved too much to bear. She had misread his slightest look as flirtation with a waitress or woman on the bus, continued to check his phone logs and emails. At every turn, Perry found himself litigating in his own defense, attempting to prove that she was mistaken, that he was not her predatory stepfather.

She would not be persuaded.

"I don't understand how the nurture and trust I offered a partner for the first time in my life provoked so much anger and suspicion."

"Focus on her pain for a moment."

This is the only way he will be able to ask the healing question.

"I can't!"

"Because your pain gets in the way."

"Yes," he nods. "If only I could get rid of this neediness, kill that part of myself…"

"You don't want to do that."

I suggest that killing feelings rather than understanding them is no solution. I remind him of the Frankel affect, the meaningful encounter with pain. In time, Perry assures me, he will be able to separate his pain from hers and at that point see everything more clearly.

I agree.

He confesses to drinking too much. I tell him to watch his dreams. "Maybe I'll go fishing."

"Good idea," I reply.

He nods, then winces on the way out—Parzival hearing the castle gate slam shut behind him.

Dressing the Wound

Perry calls two weeks later for an appointment. He hasn't had the energy for a session before this, but is determined not to run away. There is too much at stake, and he feels something important coming to the surface. He's ready to talk about his dreams, and one in particular. I look forward to the meeting. Perry's unconscious is often visionary, personal issues enriched by archetypal content. When we meet, he's clearly excited to disclose its latest message to him.

Facing me from the couch, his back ramrod straight, he recounts the dream that brought him here this afternoon.

I'm standing in front of a green curtain that slowly transforms into a face, one I find frightening. At first it is mostly a large mouth, like a tear in the fabric, except it grows lips. Then the other features press against the surface as if they are trying to fix themselves but can't. The surface is wrinkled like an old cloth. Then it becomes transparent and parts. I hesitate but can't do anything else than step through it and find myself in a cave. There's a waterfall at the far end. It falls into a pool, the kind where wild animals come to drink. There may even by footprints at the edge. Then I notice a fountain at the center of the cave. Water spills down four staggered round bowls into a catch basin. The sound of water falling surrounds me. Musical, almost harmonic.

With so much water and stone, the cave isn't damp. On the contrary, I can feel a breeze which is surprisingly dry and sweet-smelling. I start to relax, even sink into a peaceful state, until I sense something watching me, a powerful presence; it seems to be everywhere. I wonder if it is malevolent, means to do me harm. I'm scared but fascinated, wait for whatever is watching me to speak. But it doesn't. There is only silence. I am stuck to the spot. Can't move. Finally, I summon the courage to call out, "Declare yourself!" As soon as I do, the whole scene fades, and I am facing the green curtain. The surface wrinkles, lips form then answers me: "I'm here!"

Perry recalls every detail. He had visited a place where his senses registered changes like seismographs. Hyperreality, he calls it. It was more vivid to him than any other place in recent memory. He wondered if what he experienced had been a form of possession and the presence he felt there with him a demon.

"What you entered," I suggest, "is a sacred space. Jung refers to it as a *temenos*."

"What's that?"

A temenos, I explain, within the psyche is an eternal dimension, a sacred space. In Bronze Age cultures, a temenos indicated a place apart, a sanctuary or sacred grove dedicated to a god. Represented archetypally as a circle squared, it is repeated architecturally in the traditional plaza—a square where (usually) four paths lead to a circular fountain at the center.

King Arthur's Round Table is the temenos at Camelot.

Perry's dream presents its archaic form in a cave. The air within smells sweet and is without dampness, though full of running water. He had discovered, and failed to recognize, the temenos within himself.

"I was terrified," recalls Perry. "Afraid I might die."

"You had a glimpse of wholeness behind nature's curtain. The green mask of the Great Mother, which you've cast as a demon, assured you from disembodied lips that she'll be there to receive you again, when you're ready."

"I guess."

"Remember what she said?"

"Sure. She said: *I'm here!*"

Gone Fishing

Perry cancels his appointment the following week. His text reads: "I'm not running away, just want to spend time trout fishing." And again: "It's the start of the season, streams are stocked. My gear is packed."

We both understand what this means. I hope that in addition to catching trout, he will pull something else out of the deep pool of his sleep. Maybe the Oxyrhynchus, the fish which the Egyptians believed swallowed the phallus of Osiris.

"'Ripeness is all,'" I text him back.

When I see him two weeks later, he reports the following dream.

Trolling with the Fisher King

I am fly-fishing in a stream surrounded by high banks of exposed roots from the trees above. Suddenly, I feel a tug at the line, pull back, set the hook, then try to reel in, but the line is heavy and appears stuck on the bottom. I give it a tug. The line becomes free, but there is a significant weight on the other end. It doesn't fight or run, but requires enormous exertion to move.

Eventually, I can see a shadow in the water and then make out this huge brook trout, many times the size of a normal one. As it comes closer, I notice there are a lot of little fish attached to it, feeding on it. When I lift him out of the water, the small fish fall away, and the trout comes up clean. I see that its nose is slightly bent, which happens to very old fish, and that it has a mouth full of razor-sharp large teeth. But I'm not scared to touch it. Maybe because it doesn't resist in any way. I lay it out gently on the bank. It doesn't try to bite me. I am confident that it won't hurt me, and my heart is suddenly full of a mixture of sadness and joy, wide open, raw, with an overpowering emotion I realize is love.

Perry shakes his head, still in the grip of that emotion. The dream unfolds of its own accord. Before he says a word, we share an understanding of this one. What he catches in the dream is no ordinary fish, but his wounded core. This ancient creature has been buried in the sunless depths of his soul all his life. It has grown old inside of him.

Swordfish, Bruno Latini, *Livre de Tresor*

Because of his determination to confront his pain, and our work together, because he is a fisherman who has kept his line in the water, the fish has been surfacing slowly and chose to emerge at this time. He will always experience it, even in a memory, as happening in the present.

The fish waits in the shadows of the stream where Perry is likely to cast his lure.

At first the creature hugs the bottom, low enough to focus on its center of gravity. Perry doesn't fight with it. He holds fast, keeps tension on the line, just enough to tire the creature on the other end. The fish resists being pulled up but eventually tires and allows it, comes forward willingly. Perry is struck by an unexpected emotion: He feels tenderness about the catch. The feeling grows stronger as he reels. He is moved by the sight of the creature's bent nose, an indication of its age.

"Very old," he repeats.

Its eyes are large black holes that glow, like one of those blind fish that live near thermal vents at extreme depths, where there is no light; it is a perfect formulation of his woundedness. The clusters of smaller fish clinging like barnacles fall away as Perry lifts it out of the water. These he recognizes as collateral conditions that fed on his pain. The creature, too, seems relieved to shed them, revealing the iridescent hues that were hidden, green and blue, suddenly visible in the daylight. This emergent embodiment of his ancient sorrow, what had been shapeless terror now given shape, makes him cry. His tears carry with them palpable relief, almost a lightness of being. He spreads his catch on the bank, whole and clean; its razor sharp teeth pose no danger to him. In the light of making so much material conscious, Perry sees through a clear lens.

He admires the fish where it lies, old, venerable, then realizes that instead of fading, the scales have grown brighter. There is an iridescent rainbow that runs from gill to tail. Moreover, what has appeared to be a hard mask underpinned by a protruding jaw have softened to suggest a kind of serenity. What he registers in the creature's blind eye pierces his heart like a blade. As Parzival discovered "piercing through" the Fisher King's pain, there is no greater intimacy than watching the accretions that feed on another's despair fall away like barnacles through your own connection to despair. Perry is convinced that he will never love anything more than he does this fish at his feet.

DAEDALUS DELIVERS

Gypsy's Diner

Back in the Incubator

I'm sitting at Nick's tasting the last of my toasted bran muffin, getting ready to record last night's dream in the notebook open beside the coffee mug veined with grime that will never wash out. There are a few regulars at the counter: an ambulance medic named Bob, a beefy man in a blue official Jacket, Yuri, whose card reads "scientific chiropractic Ukrainian masseur," and the old man who makes duck noises. Outside, homeless men fresh from the shelter on Third Street make their way slowly down Second Avenue, find empty doorways, talk to themselves in front of the Emigrant Savings Bank on the other side of the street.

I remember last night's dream clearly, a fragment, but as if it were a lived experience—as real as my memories of Vietnam or my Brooklyn childhood around the corner from Ebbets Field.

I am looking at a man walking quickly from Gem's Spa toward Houston Street along Second Avenue. He is casually dressed in jeans and a black sweatshirt on the front of which is embossed in white block letters the legend: "Daedalus Delivers." I note his purposeful walk and repeat the words on his sweatshirt, then conclude that he is a messenger on a mission. I repeat the phrase, "Daedalus Delivers." Then answer: "And he does."

It will take me months, maybe years, to understand that the messenger is the message of this dream. As such, the dream possesses an origin and an intention, a way of delivering the message. Everything speaks of an intelligence at work that is independent of our own, what Jung refers to as the Objective Psyche and the Romans understood too as the Genius. Here, the intelligence alludes to itself as Daedalus, the mythic craftsman who constructed the labyrinth on Crete to contain the Minotaur.

The Archaeology of Dreams

It is a dream that comments on itself in a way that is counter-intuitive—suggests that it's a labyrinth which conceals something that may be monstrous or grotesque—that it contains a dangerous core-meaning buried beneath the heart of the city better left unrevealed. Or maybe it points to a fatal variable we fail to see. The tragedy doesn't lie in confronting the danger where it waits in the dark, but the attempt to escape a more encompassing captivity. Daedalus, the inventor of wings that simulate those of birds, can carry one as in a dream high above the ground. On the other hand, pursuing the dream of escape on such wings offers a perilous power for those who, like Icarus, are temperamentally unsuited to flight and unable to follow the instruction to fly neither too high nor too low. And that becomes the message of my Daedalus walking along 2nd Avenue, his feet firmly on the ground, to fly neither too high nor too low on the wings that promise to free me.

This dream has survived four decades undiminished for me. Attached to it is the smell of old urn coffee, and another artificer, Nick, guardian of my morning ritual in the temenos that is his diner. The Racing Form from which he seldom looks up challenges him daily with the riddle of fate vs. freewill, what can be calculated and what escapes the scope of probability. Seated at the Formica table, I record images from my night-sea journey. I make calculations as I set them down as to which ones will take me all the way. Nick does the same reviewing the odds on his ponies. I feel we share this purpose, as well as unspoken war wounds.

Serpentarius

Many are sustained by the promise that sooner or later, trolling the unconscious, those waters will yield what they must see. A few, like Perry, fish only to feel the late afternoon breeze and watch light dance on the stream.

There's no faith or institution necessary, nor any need to convince another who has experienced it that there is an intelligence which shapes our dreams. This is the secret conveyed by the serpent said to have licked Asclepius' ears clean and why the serpent remains wreathed around the healing staff. My dream at Nick's named that intelligence Daedalus, after the Greek artificer. Jung referred to it as the Objective Psyche, or the Self—

77

the voice from the underworld speaking through us, that Olson says "was differently heard// as, in another time..."

We fish for the creature that swallowed Osiris' phallus, the ancient one, Perry's unconscious suffering spread out on the bank, fished up from the depths that shocks us into recognition. Every morning, I write down what I've found in the tangled net of sleep, as I have done for over 50 years after returning from Vietnam. I can taste the toasted bran muffin passed over to my waiting hand across the counter by Nick, in his white apron, greet the wordless welcome of his watery blue eyes.

CONSTELLATING THE NET:
A QUANTUM FAIRYTALE

The Spiritual Pilgrim Discovering another World (Woodcut) 17th Century

"When one analyses the pre–conscious step to concepts, one always finds ideas which consist of 'symbolic images.' The first step to thinking is a painted vision of these inner pictures whose origin cannot be reduced only and firstly to the sensual perception but which are produced by an 'instinct to imagining' and which are re– produced by different individuals inde-pendently, i.e. collectively… But the archaic image is also the necessary predisposition and the source of a scientific attitude. To a total recognition belong also those images out of which have grown the rational concepts."

Wolfgang Pauli, ATOM & ARCHETYPE

SEA TIME

In my 20s, as a merchant marine crossing both oceans and several seas, I spent hours at the rail watching the relationship between sea and sky. At times they existed peacefully, like sleeping lovers, fused, with no defining horizon. Afloat in seamless space, I glimpsed the plenitude of timelessness. More often, water and air colluded in creating spellbinding iterations of light. Most incredible were their sudden declarations of war. And with each shift of mood between these elements, I identified a corresponding one in myself so that concentrated thus, in the floating world around and inside of me, the only anchor on which I could rely was the observing eye that contained imagery linking both worlds.

Crossing from San Francisco to Vietnam, by way of the Philippines, in late August 1965, the first week out held the kinds of wonders one glimpses when the waters are calm and the sky responds with amplitudes of light at all hours dancing on its surface. Sea-spouts rose between mothering ocean and covering air, sunlit ladders for angels at midday, shadow columns at dusk supporting a diaphanous Parthenon. Seabirds threading our wake. Flying fish leaping where our bow sliced the water. Suddenly, in the middle of the Pacific, the mood changed.

Wind-driven clouds drawing strength from the water became black vectors, magnitudes of size and velocities of disorienting forces. Thunder and lightning of Olympian proportion set up a fierce exchange. The order came down through the bosun to batten down the hatches. We spent the next two weeks sealed inside steel bulkheads. The storm that raged around us was Shakespearean, the kind that battered ships and scattered sailors to unknown islands. The situation had the most startling effect on me, one I couldn't explain. Only to observe that it drew me more powerfully than all the days, sights and moods that preceded it since we weighed anchor in Alameda and passed under the Golden Gate.

Every day, at the height of the turbulence, as the S.S. Esparta plunged and rolled, I made my way to the end of the shaft alley past the spinning cylinders that drove our twin screws. Where the alley narrowed, and the polished shafts disappeared into the world outside, a narrow metal ladder bolted to the bulkhead extended straight up to the main deck. I climbed it, rung by rung, from my engine room station five stories below to a small hatch at the top. It was the only unsecured one on the ship. I raised it, braced its weight against my shoulder, and peeked out to gauge the strength and direction of the wind, then, when I judged it safe, raised it all the way and climbed out. The hatch opened on the fantail, behind the paint locker, which afforded minimal protection and a modicum of secrecy. Hidden from prying eyes, I held on to the rails along the paint locker, until I lurched to the stern, where I grasped the railing around the fantail for dear life.

Twice a day, for 10 or 15 minutes, I watched as skyscraper swells lifted our twin-screw refrigerator ship like a bathtub toy. It rose so high on the swell I could see the top of mountain ranges, Appalachians, Ozarks, Adirondacks—shapes carved in stone—for an immutable instant before we dropped. The descent was as steep as it was sudden. At the bottom, nothing existed but the trough and the black, white-veined liquid marble wall that loomed like a canyon overhead.

Those who spend time at sea, out of sight of land, can tell you that there is a quality in which time and space, inner and outer, dissolve and that the experience extends beyond becoming conscious of a particular moment to becoming consciousness itself. On the ship's fantail, I did not so much witness the spectacle as participate in it. From that point of view, I apprehended the world through feeling and intuition, and the images they provided as guides, contained by the observing eye that links the individual psyche to the world soul.

It has proved to be the same position at this end of my life's arc. I stand in the stern of a boat loaded with ghosts, beside the Fisher King in his hoodie, surrounded by light bearers, in the silence of all that has been and will be, waiting for a tug at the end of a line adrift in the waters of an uncharted sea.

FISH TALK

Framing the Question

Gott ist tot, announced Nietzsche in "The Gay Science" in 1882. On the centennial year of 1900, Freud's *The Interpretations of Dreams* revealed a hole in waking consciousness full of hidden meaning, dark fears and desires, repressed instinctive material. What we walled off in order to protect civilization had spilled from the divided Victorian psyche as Mr. Hyde, Frankenstein, Dracula, and Jack the Ripper. Almost unnoticed, gods from Olympus, Sinai, Ararat, Meru, Kailash, Machu Pichu and Zion were sucked into the black hole of the cultural unconscious. By 1929, C.G. Jung observed that

> the gods have become diseases; Zeus no longer rules Olympus but rather the solar plexus, and produces curious specimens for the doctor's consulting room, or disorders the brains of politicians and journalists who unwittingly let loose psychic epidemics on the world. (Introduction to *The Secret of the Golden Flower.*)

Cronus, who attempted to devour his Olympian children lest they displace him, might find it ironic that we succeeded where he failed. Quite inadvertently, according to Jung, we have swallowed the same mythological offspring. Suppressed by new orders, or languishing in the indifference of old ones, the archetypal energies represented by the gods ceased to be "alive" as identifiable objects in the outer world. No longer to be summoned by name in rituals or prayer, they withdrew into the personal unconscious to be expressed in a variety of somaticized disorders—whole Pantheons translated into stress-related clinical symptoms.

Gertrude Stein made clear that the rate of change in the 20th century was greater than in all of those preceding it. The speed exerts a G-force equivalent to that which affects astronauts in rockets attempting to burst free of Earth's atmosphere. We have yet to

Fish Map #3, Wayne Atherton

understand the long-range effects, how this may change us as a species. But it is also true that the function and structure of the deep psyche haven't changed since our ancestors painted images on rock walls where the sun never shines. The cave of our unconscious and its content is as rich in imagery as those at Lascaux and Trois Freres. We visit this Paleolithic space in dreams. Mythic figures come and go, accompanied by emotions that make our waking ones pale. Vestiges of these immemorial images survive in comic books, cartoons, video games, niche marketing campaigns and cinematic special effects—simulations of awe. Certain image-rich fairy tales and cartoons stir the unconscious. I am thinking of "The Last Unicorn," "The Dark Crystal," "The Triplets of Belleville," the Slavic "Baba Yaga," and Hans Christian Andersen's "The Little Mermaid."

Archetypal figures emerge in apocalyptic high-relief like the emotionally compelling robots in films like "Blade Runner" and "The Terminator," or the perplexing amalgam of human and machine called Darth Vader, or in disguise as Robin Williams in "The Fisher King."

In my own life, the most powerful archetype has been Amfortas, the Fisher King. Certainly the G-force rate of change over the last 200 years has had an impact upon him. In my proximity to him on the stern of his small boat, I still can't see the face hidden beneath the cowl of his black hoodie. I imagine, too, that as Jung suggests, he may have been internalized along with all the other defrocked archetypes and now exists as a stress-related clinical symptom. It occurs to me that I may have only partially ingested him. But what has not changed is the way he addresses his pain, by fishing. Which is why I fish with him, and our skiff is full.

Amfortas is every fisherman. In spite of unforgiving changes in the world around us, the waters of the imagination spontaneously produce images often replete with their own interior light, that phosphorescence that glows most mightily where no sun shines. As a child, I imagined reeling in the rainbow from the semi-stagnant pond in Prospect Park and sensed that miraculous world below in stories read to me, like those by the Brothers Grimm and Alexander Pushkin.

Even now, I occasionally pull up a talking fish.

In Pushkin's poem, "The Tale of the Fisherman and The Fish" (1835), an impoverished Fisherman catches a golden fish in his net who begs for his life. The Fisherman, moved by his plea, throws him back. But the Fisherman's Wife, after hearing about this encounter, sends her husband back to ask the fish to grant a wish in return. The fish grants the Fisherman's first wish of a house to replace their hovel. Not satisfied with the house, she sends her husband back repeatedly with an increasingly grandiose list of wishes. Along the way, his wife becomes a queen and then a *tsarina* and finally the Ruler of the Sea in order to subjugate the fish to her will. In an earlier version of this folk tale collected by the Brothers Grimm and published in 1812 as "The Fisherman and His Wife," the fish, a flounder, claims to have been an enchanted Prince but offers to grant the fisherman a wish in return for his life. The wife in an ongoing series of demands moves from a hovel to a castle surrounded by untold wealth. Her queenly crown is replaced by a papal miter, and then the unvarnished demand that she become God. At that point, the fisherman and his wife in both stories are cast back down into their original condition.

There are a couple of minor but noteworthy differences in these two versions.

Pushkin describes a goldfish, while in the Grimm tale it is an enchanted Prince turned into a flounder. One Fisherman mistakes the gold color for the promise of material wealth. The other one is blind to the omen that he is destined to flounder. Both fail to discriminate between the visible fish as a magical wish-granting function and the unseen power it draws on. In spite of the fact that both couples have been living on what they draw from the sea, they make no conscious connection to what lies beneath the surface. With every new demand to grant a wish, the sea becomes increasingly disturbed. The princely flounder leaves a trail of blood as it sinks to the bottom.

One can't help but feel for the wounded fish, and the increasingly bloody body of water that shelters it. Any connection to the submerged source of abundance has been eclipsed by the greed of the fisherman and his wife.

Impoverishment and greed remain at the end what they were at the beginning. No one is changed by the narrative—except perhaps the reader. Andersen and Pushkin have given us a cautionary tale: those who mistake the talking fish for the source of its power are in the end impoverished. This disconnection between the fish and the fisherman may be more important than what appears to be the moral center of the tale.

What does this mean for the Fisher King? Will we grow numb to his wound and lose connection to him in the deep psyche? Will he simply ride metastatically through our liver, kidneys and lungs? On the other hand, if we locate him in our heart, might he fish up a new image to reconnect us—a quantum fairy tale?

JE SUIS QUELQUE JE TROUVE

According to Aristotle, we gain knowledge not by talking about horses, but by direct contact with a particular horse; feeling its material qualities rooted in our sense-perception leads to an intuitive grasp of the universal in the particular, its *horseness*. Empathy and intuition as ways of knowing build on a degree of participation in what it is to be the other. Aristotle based this on the notion that our souls shared a "nurturing" aspect with all living things. This can be observed in early childhood development. As infants, we learn to read the world through what we see mirrored back at us in those responsible for our nurture. This early "mirroring" experience may explain why empathy and intuition, the handmaidens of inductive reasoning, remain relevant epistemological tools. These give us a feel for correspondences and probabilities that inform us in the present day and throughout our lives —what F. David Peat refers to as "the indivisibility of consciousness, humanity and nature."

On the other hand, early mirroring may not inoculate us against advances in technology. Fractal geometry, spectroscopic measurements, nanophotonics, particles that exist for femtoseconds, three-dimensional and holographic imaging—these are information systems that break down the object of knowledge into unrecognizable components. What happens to "knowing" when we deconstruct the mirroring face of nature and it becomes possible to understand a horse or a storm at sea most efficiently as a series of algorithms?

C.G. Jung posited that we get to know our world through four basic functions, two of which are primary and two supportive. On the (primary) vertical axis "thinking" and "feeling" are in opposition, while on the (supportive) horizontal axis "sensation" and "intuition" occupy opposite sides. Each of the four provides a specialized stream of intelligence. According to this paradigm, one function on each axis develops at the expense of the other; one becomes "dominant" and the other "inferior." Extreme imbalance can create serious issues.

If a culture elevates "thinking/sensation" and diminishes the importance of "feeling/intuition," then the ability to incorporate *value* and *connection* as essential components of knowledge may diminish or even atrophy. One can't underestimate the importance of nurture in the formation of empathy in the relationship between parent and child or relating to domestic animals. Empathy as the engine of cognitive development is apparent to anyone working with young students in the classroom. When mirroring nurture is replaced by video games and cognitive development is harnessed to information gathering, the ability to read each other deeply becomes grotesquely distorted or ceases to exist. Inner and outer landscapes mirror each other; without nurture, both will become a Wasteland.

Navigating the Numen

Quantum prophet Werner Heisenberg concluded that we cannot observe phenomena without affecting them. His work on a subatomic level indicated that the movement of matter/energy responds to our consciousness. He also noted that we could calculate the speed or position of a particle, but not both. At least in that arena, it appeared that enthroned analytical intelligence had reached the limits of measurement and calculation. After his pronouncement in 1927, we were left with probability rather than certainty in our ability to predict the behavior of the fundamental elements of our world.

On the other hand, Heisenberg's observation suggests a backdoor to Aristotle's theory of knowledge encapsulated in the experience of *"horseness,"* where we once again are participants in the exploration, not simply witnesses of it. But just how can we apply our elusive understanding of subatomic particles to knowing the horse, or, to put it another way, how does one participate in what one can't see? Hopefully, imagination helps us to bridge these worlds and move past the analytics that would disconnect matter from energy. Einstein employed "thought experiments" as an essential part of his process, as a way to translate patterns and ideas inaccessible to the normal senses into visual imagery.

Here is a train moving past a station. I am both inside the train and standing on the platform. If there is a flash of light at the center of the car inside the train, I will see it at the same time from both points of view but experience the event differently. From inside the car, the flash will appear at the center. From the platform, it will appear to be moving to the rear of the car.

This difference in perception of a simultaneous event, according to the relative position of the observer, though the speed of light remained constant, proved what Einstein called his special theory of relativity. As in a dream state, he needed to see the event from both points of view at the same time. The exercise invites the imagination (which one might argue already operates according to the laws of special relativity) into a participatory experience.

Einstein's waking reveries allowed him to use his complete sensorium to experience the operations of his imagination as in a lucid dream. We respond differently to dream images that arise autonomously in sleep as if from a separate intelligence. Often there's no waking memory of what's been seen under these conditions. Many dismiss what they remember as fragmentary or irrelevant. For others, the intelligence, embedded in these autonomous images that flesh our dreams, opens the doors of perception. Einstein spoke reverentially of intuition as a guide to this process.

Developing a relationship with the intelligence that creates dreams, visions and epiphanies requires finesse. An attitude of trust deepens the connection. As in any relationship, this is usually based on experience of the benefits and our willingness to accept a degree of uncertainty. Fully grasping the content of a given dream may be like trying to know both the speed and position of an electron at the same time—a mathematical impossibility. On the other hand, we can evaluate the truthfulness or intention of the

Angelus Novus, Paul Klee

image- and symbol-forming function only when we recognize its psychological products as facts, demonstrable and undeniable.

In my practice as a psychotherapist, I encounter this repeatedly in a variety of ways. Recently, my 25-year-old client, Nick, an artist of considerable talent, related that I appeared in his dream in a wheelchair. It was at the opening of a solo exhibition of his work. He welcomed me, told me how glad he was that I had come, then asked how I was feeling. I replied: *"The world is dangerous. The world is thoughtful. I'm all right."* The words resonated deeply for him, but equally, if not more so, to me. They summed up an attitude in moving forward that, in fact, I hoped to model for him in the course of our work. Understood in this way, the dream remains a concrete visual reference point and, as such, may be viewed as a psychological fact.

A Memphite tablet from pre-dynastic Egypt 5,100 years ago tells us the creation of the world and everything in it issued from Ptah's invisible heart-thoughts, which become visible to the mind's eye before they are materialized in his spoken word. "Every divine word has come into existence through the heart's thought and the tongue's command…"

Thought takes shape in the dark, becomes visible to the mind, before it incarnates in material form and subject to its laws. So I read the message of Paul Klee's *Angelus Novus,* who, stopped in mid-descent, can't escape the object of his contemplation—Walter Benjamin called it "the Angel of History." I contemplate the message in my client's dream:

> *The world is dangerous*
> *The world is thoughtful*
> *I'm all right.*

Prehensile Precognition

Problems arise when we find ourselves beyond the ability of the imagination to form a picture of thought. The Higgs boson "God Particle" in quantum physics couldn't be seen but was intuited in 1960 as necessary to explain subatomic behavior. Forty years later, its existence has been tentatively confirmed by the CERN accelerator. In 1930, Nobel Laureate Wolfgang Pauli expressed the hope that he would live to see the invisible "thought" he named the *neutrino.*

It became visible in 1956 at a nuclear reactor on the Savannah River. Pauli died in 1958, two years later, without seeing his offspring.

Today the *neutrino* is thought to be essential to the cohesion of particles but is unconstrained by any of the laws that govern them; lacking an electrical charge, neutrinos pass through great distances in matter without being affected by it. They leave no footprint. Put another way, the *neutrino* remains unimaginable.

DESCENDING ANGELS

Pauli's Ladder

At age 24, Austrian-Swiss theoretical physicist Wolfgang Pauli (1900-1958) had established The Pauli Exclusion Principle, which set forth a theory of "spin" to explain the way electrons behaved inside an atom. It also established stability in intense magnetic fields such as in neutron stars, calculated the hydrogen spectrum and posited the existence of the *neutrino*.

Pauli's principle, in sum, revealed the structure of matter and predicted the death of stars. In spite of these achievements, the Nobel Prize genius spent much of his life in quantum physics desperately unhappy. Pauli worked closely with Neils Bohr and Werner Heisenberg to formulate basic quantum theory as part of the Copenhagen Experiment in

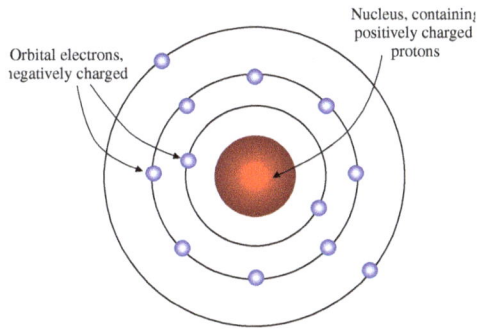

Bohr's Model Atom, Usnw, Australia

1924. At that time, challenges posed by the hitherto unknown subatomic world were galvanized by discoveries like "complementarity," the dual nature of energy as both particle and wave elaborated by Bohr in 1928. These waters were as uncharted as any crossed by Europeans in the 15th century on their way to the New World.

Physicists on the subatomic ocean also felt most comfortable close to shore, where the flora and fauna of the imagination provided a template. But even Einstein's early "thought experiments" were less available to them as they sailed farther from land into a featureless sea. It proved to be a daunting journey. Without the imagination and its productions, it seems we are lost in deep space, directionless in utter darkness.

Images, geometries and analogies anchor us.

How much more vivid deep space becomes if we compare it to a Paleolithic cave. Spinning galaxies and stellar explosions become the photonic equivalents of bison and wooly mammoth emblazoned on its walls. Physicist/astronomer Sir James Jeans wrote in 1930, *the universe begins to look more like a great thought than like a great machine. Mind no longer appears as an accidental intruder into the realm of matter; we are beginning to suspect that we ought rather to hail it as a creator and governor of the realm of matter...*

Bad Behavior

Mind and matter imagine themselves as each is mirrored by the other. In this way, they remain comprehensible to us. Pauli challenged that when he questioned Bohr's image of the atom as a planetary system. The last thing he wanted to do was destabilize that structure, but what he observed in the behavior of electrons made it impossible for him to do otherwise.

Pauli's assault on Bohr's atomic theory was inadvertent and devastating.

In his attempt to answer the questions raised by Bohr's solar model, Pauli moved away from it. Along the way, he formulated Pauli's Exclusion Principle, which established "spin" as a property of the electron. The fact that electrons "spin" in opposite directions explained why they didn't collapse in a heap. Not gravity-based, planetary spin doesn't operate inside the atom. Subatomic "spin" does but is impossible to visualize.

Pauli's "spin" accounted for so much. Among other things, it dissolved any possibility of an inert core (sun) at the center of orbiting electrons. By 1925, it was clear that Bohr's model of the atom could no longer be sustained. The existence of the atom in its new incarnation had become a fact. It was also, all agreed, unimaginable.

Arthur I. Miller's book, *137, Jung, Pauli, and the Pursuit of a Scientific Obsession,* describes the reaction of Pauli and his colleagues to the loss of the image. Visual support for atomic theory had provided a shared experience. In its absence, the void beckoned. The situation triggered depression in Pauli and created anxiety in his colleagues—especially Bohr.

They tried to comfort each other.

Pauli expressed his hope that eventually quantum theory would make visual sense of these ideas. "Once systems of concepts are settled," he told Bohr, "then will visualizability be regained." (62)

Even as he grieved over what had been lost, Pauli moved forward. The products of his own formidable intelligence haunted him, and often for the same reason. His conceptual reach moved beyond his imaginal grasp. As he would say about his notion of the *neutrino*: "I have done a terrible thing. I have postulated a particle that cannot be detected."

Aware that imagination was giving way to numbers, Einstein wrote, "There is no logical path to these laws; only intuition, resting on sympathetic understanding of experience can reach them." He was talking about the only way he knew to glimpse "the 'pre-established' harmony of the universe." (93) With the collapse of Bohr's solar model, atomic physics seemed to lie in ruins.

> I have done a terrible thing, I have postulated a particle that cannot be detected.
>
> *Wolfgang Pauli*

Arthur Miller writes about this turning point in intellectual history: "It was time for atomic physics to move on from trying to visualize everything in images relating to the world in which we live." Heisenberg put the fine point on it when he suggested that as scientists, and perhaps as a species linked by an interconnected field of consciousness, we had moved into an area of nature that defied imagination.

Wolfgang Pauli, cast adrift in a wilderness bereft of images, questioned everything he had once thought worthy in his list of achievements. In this quantum arena where particle and wave are interchangeable, he played both Parzival and Amfortas. Like Parzival after the banquet, Pauli wrapped himself in a cloak of wounded pride. As Amfortas, he watched Parzival disappear into the night, aware that it might be years before such an opportunity appeared again.

FRAMING THE QUESTION

From Wolfram to Wolfgang

Finally, it is Pauli as the Fisher King who emerges overall, a one-time Grail keeper disconnected by the unhealed wound of his own devising. At a time when physics and psychology were undergoing a sea change, the boundary between them ever more unclear, few have fished more passionately for what is hidden beneath the surface. Perhaps we can best grasp the *Geist* of this period in astrological terms, the movement of the equinox as it shifts from Pisces to Aquarius. In Pisces we swam like fish in the ocean of the unconscious. As Aquarians, we hold the amphora dispensing the element that once contained us. It is in the course of this transition that Pauli sails into the unimaginable.

The loss of the imaginal function to the physics of the time stunned the Quantum Knights as they sat at the roundtable staring at their shields. For the time being, they could only express ideas as equations. Pauli, the Fisher King, confided in his Parzival surrogate, Werner Heisenberg, *We must adjust our concepts to experience.* Standing resolutely at the stern, an exacting critic of his floundering peers, Pauli became known to them as "God's whip," even as his personal life went into a downward spiral.

In 1927, Pauli's mother, Bertha, a brilliant journalist, poisoned herself in response to his father's desertion following an extramarital affair. Pauli's marriage to a cabaret performer proved stormy and short-lived. Back in Zurich, he went on drinking binges. His forays into the bars became increasingly violent, and he began to argue with colleagues at the university. He might easily have been mistaken for Fredrick March in the hit movie of 1931 *Dr. Jekyll and Mr. Hyde*. He may have started off as a Gold Fish at 24, but at 30, like the Princely Flounder in Grimm's fairy tale version, Pauli sank to the bottom, trailing blood and the invisible *neutrino*.

In danger of losing everything, he sought help from C.G. Jung, whose vision of the collective unconscious mirrored Pauli's understanding of the quantum universe. The relationship between the conscious and the unconscious in Jung's psychology was analogous to that of particle and wave in Pauli's physics. Working with Jung, Pauli recovered the application of his powerful imagination in the existence of the archetypes. These constellated patterns of energy could be expressed in physical form. Pauli used them to reclaim the sense-experience that had been lost to the unimaginable implications of quantum physics.

Through the language of symbols that emerged in his dreams, Pauli once again harnessed the image-making faculty to his formidable analytic abilities in mapping out new terrain shared by science and psychology. It was as though someone had whispered in his ear the answer to a question that had held him hostage for many years. Confronting what had seemed an irresolvable existential conflict, Pauli's dream image of the World Clock crystalized his ideas and intuition about the mystery of eternity unfolding in time in a living symbol.

Briefly Mapping the Terrain

In Bronze Age cultures, a temenos was recognized as a sanctuary, usually dedicated to a god.

Carl Jung linked its basic shape, repeated in traditional plazas where (usually) four paths converge on a circular fountain at the center, to spiritual iconography as the Mandala, a symbol of wholeness, the circle squared. His insistence on the temenos as a psychological fact was supported by its measureable recurrence in the physical world.

This potential for physical/psychological equivalents in the quantum arena is more elusive.

Though subatomic processes are said to more closely resemble a great mind than a machine, the absence of direct physical analogies makes it harder to insist on them as indications of an indivisible consciousness. Consider the *neutrino*: Lacking an electrical charge, the neutrino moves through matter without creating a ripple but in theory holds the constituents of the material world together. There is a high level of ambiguity in representing the *neutrino*, as one might the temenos, as a physical/psychological fact.

My client Perry, a 50-year-old man, suddenly abandoned by the only women in years to capture his heart, dreamed of parting a green curtain to find himself in a cave configured like a classic Mandala—he had discovered the temenos within himself. Pauli's apprehension of the *neutrino* and Perry's encounter with the temenos were experienced by senses interior to those we use when awake. Pauli remained uneasy about the absence of an image for the object of his knowledge. How could he fully know what he couldn't see, even guided by his profound intuition. As Gertrude Stein pointed out after returning to Oakland, California, and finding her childhood home gone: *There is no there there.*

Symbols like the temenos that bridge inner and outer worlds convey a comforting sense of a realized intention. The naked intuition of the *neutrino*, on the other hand, alludes to a darker, impersonal mystery. Intuition in isolation became for Pauli an unendurable wound. In his work with Jung, trolling the waters of the unconscious, Pauli found his way back to the symbol- forming intelligence. The World Clock surfaced like a talking fish during his early years of dream analysis with Jung. In this fairy tale, the man who stripped subatomic physics of visual equivalents, fished up an image that linked deep psyche to the creation of stars.

TELLING TIME

The Invisible Number

Pauli's focus on dreams drew him into the mystery of archetypal representations and their transformative power; trolling these waters eased his pain. It also strengthened his conviction: The intelligence embedded in the unconscious, not logic, connected us to what Einstein called "the 'pre- established' harmony of the universe." Ideas that knit the atom to the cosmos could be developed mathematically and tested in equations, but mathematical formulae could never explain the mystery of consciousness or account for intui-

TRIUSQUE COSMI MAIORIS,
Robert Fludd

tion. Pauli continued to flesh out his ideas with the symbolic language of mysticism, alchemy and archetypes in consultation with Jung and independently for the next 26 years.

Pauli and Jung co-authored a book, *The Interpretation of Nature and the Psyche,* to probe the connection between science and psychology. In it, they explored the notion of synchronicity, or "meaningful coincidence," and its subatomic equivalent, "entanglement," where two or more particles with nothing connecting them exhibit identical behaviors—what Einstein called "spooky action at a distance."

No better example of this phenomenon could be found than in what became known as the Pauli Effect, witnessed with some regularity by a number of people on various occasions over the years. When Wolfgang Pauli walked into a laboratory, test tubes shattered, beakers exploded and objects fell off the shelves. There have been a number of theories put forth to explain this, among them his almost palpable stress-driven intensity and an overly active pineal gland.

Synchronicity dogged Pauli's footsteps, as Arthur Miller points out in his fine study, *137*.

Pauli's mentor Arnold Sommerfeld discovered the number 137 as the value of the "fine structure" of light emitted and absorbed by atoms. Along with the fingerprint, or DNA, of each wavelength, 137 emerged as a dimensionless fundamental constant in nature, central to relativity and quantum theory and necessary to the existence of life. It is also the numerical sum of Hebrew letters in the word "Cabbala." Pauli found the number resoundingly archetypal and linked to ancient wisdom traditions. Einstein and the Zohar employ "intuition resting on sympathetic understanding," as a way to read the book of the world in number and symbol. 137, the constant of underlying unity, was such a number, and perhaps a symbolic equivalent for the Holy Grail. Long before a similar narrative was created by Douglas Adams around the number 42 in his *Hitchhiker's Guide to the Galaxy*, when questioned by a colleague as to what he might ask God if the opportunity arose, Pauli answered, "Why 137?"

On Friday, December 5, 1958, Pauli collapsed while teaching, then complained of stomach pains. He was transported to the Red Cross Hospital in Zurich, where a friend, Charles Enz, who had accompanied him, noticed that Pauli was agitated. When he asked why, Pauli indicated the number above the door. He had been placed in room 137 and announced to his friend quite accurately that he would not be leaving it alive. After the removal of a massive pancreatic carcinoma, on December 15 Pauli died in Room 137.

Ending on a Synchronistic Note

Given his interest in time and obsession with the fine structure constant, Pauli felt that his dream image of The World Clock supplied a visual resolution to questions that remained open. For him it captured the mystery of the unified field. It might have amused him to learn that according to the calculation yielded by the Hubble Space Telescope measuring the speed at which galaxies are moving—that is, the age of the Universe—the time elapsed since the Big Bang is currently calculated at 13.7 billion years.

WINDING THE WORLD CLOCK

Parting the Waves

Wolfgang Pauli always felt incomplete as a scientist. Even though the Pauli Exclusion Principle revealed the structure of matter and predicted the deaths of stars, the exploration that measures its conclusions in vanishing traces of light and particles left him adrift. Pauli spent his life in pursuit of a disembodied science that, according to Heisenberg, defied imagination. While Heisenberg's uncertainty at the quantum banquet would make a significant contribution to framing the important questions, Pauli had earlier realized the unimaginable, a state beyond which there was no correlative physical image or symbol to hold the idea. He responded to it by splitting in half.

The professor who tail-walked quantum waves by day turned by night into a dark figure who raged in bars and brothels. Pauli might have split definitively had he not found a temenos in Jung's psychology. It felt familiar from the start. But Jung's vision gave a shape to what Pauli had intuited as a scientist—an equivalence between the unconscious and the quantum universe: "Even the most modern physics lends itself to symbolic representations of psychic process."

Certain critics suggested that Jung manipulated his subjects to produce the archetypal dream material. He took a pre-emptive approach to his work with Pauli by making sure the content of Pauli's dreams was "... absolutely pure, without any influence from myself." For this reason, when Pauli entered treatment, Jung assigned him to a fledgling student of his, Erna Rosenbaum.

During five months with Rosenbaum, Pauli retrieved hundreds of dreams. Jung found the symbols that appeared in them similar to those in Medieval Alchemy. Jung chose 400 of Pauli's 1,300 dreams for his research into alchemical symbolism in the modern psyche. Quite apart from Jung's research, Pauli probed his own symbol production with detailed notes and illustrations. In these notes he describes the experience of "sublime harmony" that accompanied his "great vision" of The World Clock.

As he predicted long ago to Bohr, once the system and concepts settle, "then will visual imagery be regained." The structure in Pauli's great vision is assembled to evoke consciousness as a process of interlocking geometries held in the mystery of the unconscious, which exists outside of space-time. Writing later of Pauli's vision that arrived on the wings of a blackbird (Hermes bird) in flight, Jung says: "It seems to be an attempt to make a meaningful whole of the formerly fragmentary symbols, then characterized as circle, globe, square, rotation, clock, star, cross, quaternity, time, and so on." He characterized the vision as proof of a "conversion."

Jung used this "religious" term to indicate the depth of Pauli's transformation: The wound that had divided his psyche was healed. This vision reconciled science and psychology, along with other formerly opposing elements of his personality, in a complex representation of cosmic harmony, the *unus mundus*. Pauli wrote Jung from Zurich in 1938: "The relationship of these images is strongly affective and connected with a feeling that could be described as a mixture of fear and awe."

Pauli's "World Clock," Beyers-Brown

Pauli writes about emerging from his vision in a peaceful state. What moved his genius to significant discoveries in quantum physics was never accompanied by such a profound sense of well-being. Pauli tells us that The World Clock brought to light "deeper spiritual layers that cannot be adequately defined by the conventional concept of time." In that moment, he produced an image that was a vehicle for transcendence. Jung describes it as "a moment when long and fruitless struggles came to an end and a reign of peace began." This sounds very much like the way Wolfram describes the function of the *lapis exilles* as that condition which reconciles opposites. With his vision of The World Clock, Pauli renewed the archetypal symbol for wholeness that reconciles particle and wave, depth psychology and quantum physics, body and mind, and time and eternity in a postmodern version of The Holy Grail.

CHANNEL FEVER

Raising the Dead

Channel Fever is a state of extreme agitation that afflicts seamen on their way into or out of the harbor. Settled on the beach, one is anxious to get back to sea. Conversely, still in the channel returning from sea, one can taste, see and smell the beach. Observable symptoms: pacing the companionways at night, painting valves and gauges in the engine room the wrong colors, compulsive masturbation and emotional lability. I recall watching an able-bodied seaman on a decrepit freighter spend an hour trying to heat a can of soup on a toaster. A more extreme case was the oiler who kept trying to go over the side while we waited for the pilot to take us into Port Newark, as though he might beat us there doing the backstroke. I ran into him a year later at the old Drum Street union hall in San Francisco. After a session with the union shrink and a brief period on disability, he was again possessed by channel fever and on his way back to sea.

Something turns inside out in those who spend days adrift in sea-time, especially fishermen on the troll. Most seamen, when given the opportunity, will throw out a line. Few would have difficulty accepting the idea that the man next to him at the rail has heard a fish talk or admit that he had been recently talking to one himself.

Years after disembarking in Seattle on my return from Vietnam to a world I didn't recognize, I discovered the writings of those who sailed the unconscious, an order of seamen who not only talked to fish, but to a range of invisibles. Jung cultivated relationships with figures in his reveries, dreams and reflections. Similar to Einstein's "thought experiments," Jung called this practice "active imagination." Both situations set up an interrogation of the psyche that allows the observer to engage the *other* outside the constraints of space-time, to participate in what is observed like the man who is simultaneously in the train and on the platform.

Getting to Know Abraxas

Notable among the imagined figures Jung cultivated was Philemon, a wise old uncle who became, over time, Jung's spirit guide. Many such encounters with archetypal figures can be found in Jung's *The Red Book*, a record of confrontations with his unconscious based on experiences between 1913 and 1917. It became the seedbed of ideas he developed over the next 45 years. In a reverie at the end of *The Red Book*, Philemon appears at Jung's door with a gathering of dead souls and informs him: *These were seekers and still hover over their graves. Their lives were incomplete, since they knew no way beyond the one to which belief had abandoned them.*

Jung revised this discourse as *Septem Sermones ad Mortuos* in a private edition for friends.

He later appended it to his autobiography, *Memories, Dreams & Reflections,* published posthumously in 1962, in which he also describes the occasion when the dead appeared to him in a reverie on Sunday, January 30, 1916. It started with a restlessness that grew into a sense of other presences filling the room. "They were packed deep right up to the door, and the air was so thick it was scarcely possible to breathe. As for myself, I was all a-quiver with the question: 'For God's sake, what in the world is this?'"

Constellating the Net: A Quantum Fairytale

Here, in Sermo II, we are introduced to a vision that lays bare the challenge of this gnosis and the key figure behind it who spans mind and matter: *This is a god whom ye knew not, for mankind forgot it. We name it by its name ABRAXAS.*

In the last version of *Seven Sermons to the Dead,* Jung's doorbell rings, and he answers it to find the Gnostic sage Basilides, who flourished in Alexandria about A.D. 125. Basilides answers Jung's question with the opening line from the Red Book:

The dead came back from Jerusalem, where they found not what they sought. They prayed me let them in and besought my word and thus I began my teaching.

Jung studied the Gnostic systems for analogies to the structure and dynamics of the psyche.

Basilides conceived of *gnosis* as light descending from an ineffable God, through a series of emanations, to become entangled in progressively more dense layers of matter. The invisible and visible worlds are separated by a limbic zone which Basilides calls the "intermediate *pneuma,*" which partakes of both worlds. If we analogize this to the operations of psyche, we might say it is the zone where light generated by the deep unconscious is broken into dreams that break through to consciousness at the threshold of mind and matter. Sparks of that light known to the mind are held in the heart. The Greeks called the soul-spark *synteresis,* which Aquinas would later link to a "knowledge of first principles."

But there are disruptions unique to our age that relativize absolutes and blur the boundaries of experience as in no other time. Today, symbols that once captured its light, like a Mark Rothko painting, may be reduced to the

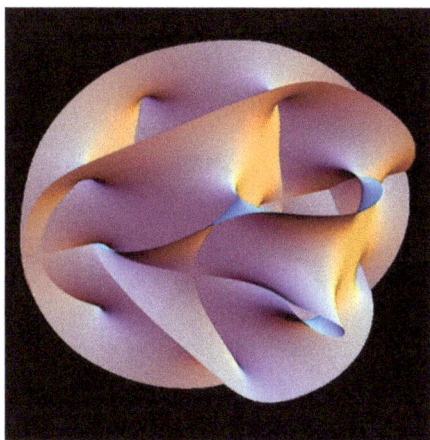

Calabi-Yau manifold, *Creative Commons*

103

size of a postage stamp. Anyone who has stood in front of a full-blown Rothko canvas and entered it recognizes that space as one of "intermediate *pneuma.*" A postage stamp of the same image will make sure only your letter gets from Glens Falls, New York, to Peoria, Illinois.

Embracing the Unimaginable: A Matter of Scale

The notion of scattered sparks of gnostic light may find an equivalent in the scattered amplitudes of particle interaction in a quantum field. It is hard to explain the most recent advance of mathematical physics. But how does one visualize the amplituhedron?

Basilides might suggest we could call it *Abraxas,* whom he identifies as *the Pleroma itself,* the potential and realization of all forms. Like the Gnostic god, the amplituhedron is an all-inclusive geometric notion that is not built out of space-time. With overtones of a new age Grail, it is described as a "multi-faceted jewel in higher dimensions" that encodes basic features of reality as "scattering amplitudes." Afloat in our moment, the existential question remains: Where in the face of unimaginable amplitude do we cast our quantum net constelled to hold the stars and the unseen properties of an entangled universe? How can we troll of the imagination with such a net?

Abraxas Anguipede,
Roman (300AD)

At Jung's door, lecturing the congregation of the dead who had journeyed to Jerusalem and failed to find what they sought, Basilides declared: *Hard to know is the deity of Abraxas.*

In the earlier draft, Philemon tells us that *Abraxas is a God mankind forgot,* though he stands above the one they remember. If Basilides were at the door today, he might simply repeat that *Abraxas is hard to hold.*

Basilides could be describing the quantum world when he tells us in Sermo II: *Abraxas is effect. Nothing stands opposed to him but the ineffective; hence his effective nature unfolds itself freely. The ineffective neither exists nor resists.* Before Heisenberg's Uncertainty Principle, there was *Abraxas. He is improbable probability, that which takes unreal effect.* The forgotten god, attributed to Basilides in the second century A.D. and channeled through Carl Jung in the 20th, is perfectly suited to a quantum world that defies imagination.

Abraxas = the *Neutrino.*

RECONFIGURING THE NET: A CONVERSATION WITH THE CATCH

The Pre-conscious Step

In my reverie, I am sitting in the crew mess and feel the rush of channel fever. I itch for solid ground. But I can't see the beach, except as a distant shore. I remember 50 years ago climbing the ladder at the end of the shaft alley to the open hatch behind the paint locker and pushing myself into the storm. Standing at the rail as the fantail rose and fell, I merged with what I saw, what links psyche to the world soul, to know the horse or a storm as Aristotle suggests we know anything, by becoming it.

Even though I can't see it clearly, I feel the ship that carries me coming into the channel. I consider raiding the "night lunch" or heating a can of soup on the toaster but understand that neither will address my hunger. I hunger to know what moves people to put a human face on transcendence, then die or kill to defend it. A hunger that verges on instinct. I hunger to be comforted by something greater than my hunger. In a world that defies imagination, I hunger for the reassurance of a fairy tale.

I leave the crew mess. Standing at the rail on the bow, I scan what is ahead. The engines slow almost to a stop. We might be preparing for the pilot to come aboard, as we must before we can dock. He will take us in. The pilot knows the currents and shoals. But his boat is nowhere in sight. I wait, eyes closed. When I open them again, I'm standing at the water's edge holding a line. It appears I have caught and released a fish.

The goldfish that pokes out of the water has Wolfgang Pauli's face, complete with the square jaw tending to jowl. He tells me that he will grant one wish and asks me what I want. I reply that I would like to pull up from the depths the answer to my most profound question, which I have not yet framed even for myself.

The Paulifish frowns, then declares he will do even better and instructs me on how to constellate a quantum-net to capture the theory of everything. I take mental notes so as to follow his directions precisely in drawing the plan.

Fish, Roman Mosaic (Israel)

When I get home, I find a pad and pencil, then draw what I remember, the directive voice clear in my head. I'm disappointed with the result. What I see on the paper looks like a newt.
I return to the shore. The Paulifish appears again.

I describe to him what happened when I followed his instruction. "I ended up with a newt, not a net."

He repeats my words, "a newt, not a net." Shakes his head. I protest again that I adhered exactly to his directions.

"You're not even wrong," he repeats his well-known response to a cowering student. Then laughs. "Newton's net is not what it used to be. I'm talking about gravity. Highly overrated in the scheme of things. Even a nitwit knows a newt is not a net."

It's not supposed to work this way, I tell him. This interchange between us is supposed to be richer, magical, a way of riddling existence.

He is somber, this Paulifish, and nods. If there is something I want from him, I must say it and stop demanding that he both ask and answer my question.

"Fair enough," I agree.

Again that smirk.

"OK," I tell him. "I want a concrete image to reveal what I know so deeply that it remains invisible to me."

"Be specific," he insists.

"I need a pilot to guide me to the harbor I can't see from the ship in my mind. And to see the ship from the beach where I now stand talking to you."

"That's two wishes," he yawns.

"I want to know the world again as once I did, in full color," I blurt. "When I could be in two different places at the same time."

Paulifish nods as best he can, considering he has no neck. He repeats the advice he gave to Bohr when his solar model for the atom went belly-up. Systems and concepts have to settle, he assured me. I will perhaps be able to visualize again what is necessary for me.

"That's not good enough," I protest. "What about my quantum net?"

Paulifish tells me it's too late to discuss this today. I might come back tomorrow. Or, better, in a week. Meanwhile, I should remember his words.

"What are those?" I ask, as if it mattered.

"Keep your line in the water."

DINNER WITH
THE FISHER KING

Toyen (Marie Cerminova): *Among the Long Shadows*

Parzival felt all the grief he had encountered since he first began his long journey into exile from true innocence of heart. And in the same moment of anguished illumination, he saw how—mile after mile, day after day, battle after battle, until he had finally met defeat at his brother's hands—that guilt driven journey had taken him further and further from the one true source of joy and meaning in his life. Reflecting on his pride and bitterness, the willful error of his ways, he found himself wondering what the wound was at the heart—or in the mind—of man that kept him forever in exile from what he most desired.

Lindsay Clarke, *Parzival and the Stone from Heaven*

FOR WHOM THE BUOY TOLLS

I had an email correspondence with Justin for several months. Although we never met face to face, he was a poet/fisherman who had spent time at sea. A mutual friend in the U.K. arranged an electronic introduction based on our common interests. Subsequently, we exchanged work by mail—our respective memoirs and poetry collections. I hoped my account of trolling for marlin in *Fishing on the Pole Star* would ring true for him.

We both grew up fishing for blues out of Sheepshead Bay, Long Island Sound and Montauk, I as a paying passenger on party boats and he as crew on his father's private charter. I was moved by the thought of him as a boy filling the ice chests, cleaning the catch, stowing gear and hosing the deck under his father's rigorous command. I considered the anger and humiliation he might have felt untangling lines, adjusting the drag of would-be anglers or gaffing a big blue before it jumped the hook. His formative years tolled in my imagination like Robbins Light, the buoy at the mouth of New York Bay.

Justin's emails to me were cool, a few words to make a point or ask a question. I was reluctant to probe him by email after reading his memoir. The personal content, presented in a formal style, left me reluctant, like Parzival at the banquet, to pursue further questions, but with more than enough information to develop a picture.

Justin was born in Sag Harbor, New York, a whaling town known to Herman Melville and a stop on the Underground Railroad. He grew up a brilliant, blue-eyed boy among a population of blue-collar locals, affluent transplants and artists escaping the city. Justin excelled in school and at the age of 18 left home without looking back. After graduating from University of Pennsylvania with a degree in finance, he spent a graduate year at Oxford. Back in the states, he worked in mergers and acquisitions before becoming a citizen of the U.K. Most of the year, he occupied an office at Oxford reserved for scholars and emeriti. Summers he spent on Martha's Vineyard. He never discussed his wealth directly, but it had to be considerable.

My young adult years were a patchwork of jobs that included shipping out, driving a cab, tending bars and stints at a number of educational institutions. I considered the years at the Tin Palace to have been my graduate school, from which I walked away with no degree, but six months of unemployment benefits. I recorded all of this in *My Brother's Madness*, the memoir I sent him as part of our exchange.

I heard nothing from him after several months. I assumed we'd said all there was to say to each other. So, his email in early April came as a surprise. Justin invited me to visit him on the weekend of August 15 at his summer home, *Ardetta Exilis*, on Martha's Vineyard. The date fell at the end of my residency at the Gloucester Writers Center.

I wrote back that my wife would be joining me in Gloucester. I already had a reading booked at the Bunch of Grapes bookstore in Vineyard Haven on Thursday, August 14. We looked forward to spending that weekend with him.

The day before I left for Gloucester, Justin sent me a message that due to an unforeseen obligation, he was no longer free for the entire weekend, but an overnight on Friday would work for him. He apologized that it couldn't be longer and hoped to see us that night for dinner.

"Let's do it," said my wife.

LEAVING GLOUCESTER

On the last night of my residency, Carol joins me in the one-room cape. She'd expected something more elaborate. We sit at the small writing table. I admire her broad cheeks, full lips, red highlights in her shoulder-length hair. She is my Queen of Cups. I point out photos of Ferrini and Olson. Imposing at 6-foot-8, Olson's physical size is proportional to his impact on American poetry and on me. From the first night, lines from his poem "The Kingfishers" have been echoing in my dreams.

What does not change / is the will to change

Carol remarks that I'd come to this fishing village, home of poet/fishermen, to read from *Fishing on the Pole Star*, my collection about fishing.

"It's almost operatic," she comments. "Bizet's *The Pearl Fishers*."

"I couldn't stop thinking about Amfortas."

"In Wagner's *Parsifal*, Amfortas is a baritone."

"Wolfram's Amfortas," I tell her. "The fisherman with a pre-existing condition."

"Parzival or Amfortas, which are you?" Carol's green eyes sparkle.

"I navigate between baritone and tenor."

A few days earlier, the 30 or so people who came to hear me read poems from *Polestar* remained when I followed with my talk, *Trolling with the Fisher King*. More than a few of my audience wore Kingfisher colors, swatches of blue and green that reminded me of Olson's line: ... *who cares /for their feathers/ now?* The question continued to resonate in my head. I repeat it aloud now to Carol.

"You do," she answered.

My seabirds had seemed more interested in the questions raised by my talk than in my work. Their attention loosened my tongue. I told them that the title of my talk had come shortly after waking from a dream on my first morning here. What I had to say about trolling with the Fisher King spilled like water out of my Aquarian unconscious. But for some reason I stopped short of confessing that in my Fisher King dream, the tall man whose face remained hidden in a black hoodie refused to speak to me.

Operatic, indeed.

On the morning of our departure, over coffee, I confess to being anxious. Leaving this place is going to be harder than I anticipated.

"What do you make of it?" Carol studies me.

"I don't want my troll to end."

I had embarked on it under Ferrini's watchful gaze and, by the end of the week, found myself on a boat full of ghosts like those who appeared with Basilides at Jung's doorstep in *Seven Sermons for the Dead*.

"What if I can't finish our discussion, never see the Fisher King's face? It could stop cold when we drive away?"

"We can't let that happen," she assured me.

Carol takes my arm. We walk to the Hyundai. As she sees it, there's no reason why my troll shouldn't continue now that it's been launched inside of me. Think of our Martha's Vineyard journey as a quest, and our final destination, *Ardetta Exilis*, as the Grail Castle.

The suggestion is comforting. We are moving into the inevitable next phase of an unfolding mystery. I slip easily into the driver's seat.

My wife repeats the name.

Ardetta Exilis.

After fastening her seat belt, Carol checks her iPad. Even before I pull out on to the road, she finds the definition she's looking for: *Ardetta Exilis* is a small wading bird similar to the heron.

IN FLIGHT

I point our silver Hyundai south. Our first stop, Boston. We will spend the night on Kenmore Square at the Buckminster Hotel, a gray stone-and-brick structure designed by Stanford White at the start of the last century. It had been the location of Storyville, a legendary '50s jazz club, where people could hear Billie Holiday, Charlie Parker, Dave Brubeck, Charles Mingus and Sarah Vaughan. It is now a Pizzeria Uno. The entrance on Brookline is framed by veined black marble. Sliding glass doors open on a lemon yellow art-deco lobby crowned with gold-leafed laurels.

After a nap, we slow-walk down Commonwealth Avenue, a boulevard divided by a verdant mall. Falling light casts a glow over the stone-and-brick buildings, their turrets, garrets and wrought-iron fences. We turn right onto Mass Ave. and again on Boylston, full of tourists and natives. On the veranda of the Atlantic Fish Company, we are lucky to score a table by the rail hedged with flower boxes. Carol and I split a salad of wild greens, roasted beets, spiced pecans and toasted goat cheese. She orders a seared North Atlantic salmon with ricotta gnocchi, andouille sausage, spinach, heirloom cherry tomatoes and a white wine-lemon pan sauce. I can't resist the seared sesame tuna served rare with sautéed bok choy. Halfway through the meal we realize that only a year earlier this place was devastated by the Boston Marathon bombing, which explains the pristine condition of the interior, wounds no longer visible. I'm less confident that they do not bleed through, unseen but cohesive as dark matter.

The following morning is overcast but burns off by that afternoon when we exit U.S. 1 toward Cape Cod. We cross the Bourne Bridge and proceed to the second exit on the roundabout to MA-28, south to Woods Hole, where we will catch the ferry to Vineyard Haven.

At the Steam Ship Authority, we wait in a line of cars to board the ferry. Once parked in the belly of the vessel, we climb three flights of stairs to the top deck. Summer residents and weekend tourists lean against rails. Seagulls cry, and the smell of salt air revives me from the fatigue that had nestled in my bones.

The invitation to read at the Bunch of Grapes came through Jay and Ivy, who summer at their house in Tisbury. They thought my *Pole Star* would attract an audience on an island populated by poets and fishermen. I'd emailed them from Gloucester about Justin's invitation for Friday night. Jay replied that Justin was entirely unknown to them, as was *Ardetta Exilis* in Menemsha Heights. When they greet us at the landing stage in Vineyard Haven, Ivy confides that no one they talked to had anything to add.

I tell them that this is because the Fisher King's castle occupies an imaginary space, a dimension that intersects with ours but can't be accessed by intention.

"Invitation only."

Trolling with the Fisher King

The Bunch of Grapes is the only year-round bookstore on the island. It caters to a local and literary population of summer dwellers, visiting U.S. presidents among them. The interior of the space on Main Street in Vineyard Haven is hedged by book cases and table displays behind lattice windows. Prominently on display are signed copies of *Boys in the Trees* by local author Carly Simon. Another island resident, historian David McCullough, has left a supply of his latest book, *The Wright Brothers*. My event is a part of their Thursday reading series that takes place in a nook at the rear. We find chairs and a couch arranged in a circle. There may be 30 people gathered. We need more chairs. My book title, *Fishing on the Polestar*, appears to have expanded the audience, more than a few of them being locals who fish commercially for blues and stripers. A few will be familiar with trolling baits in formations in the pursuit of billfish, most often marlin. I alert them that I will be reading from a metaphysical work that uses fishing as a metaphor. No one takes this seriously until I read the poem "Marlin Strike."

It describes a moment, after weeks on the troll, just beyond Concepcion Island, when I hook a 300-pound marlin, fight him for two hours, and then bring him to the starboard side. Our mate holds him in place to "swim him," quiet the creature and move him slowly until the water circulating through his gills restores color depleted after our struggle. No shark in the ocean can best a marlin in full bloom. Dimmed, he is doomed.

Our big boy allows us to swim him until bands of green and blue blossom the length of his body. Then he bites down gently on the hand of the man who is holding him to signal he's ready. The power in his great jaws could take the arm of his handler off at the shoulder with little effort—but the touch is delicate, almost reverential. Upon release, he rides up over the gunnel to meet our eyes. What I see in that perfect roundness of marlin's eye, an intelligence so balanced, so complete, takes my breath away.

For a second, I glimpse the Divine Child, *the constant which links the atom to the stars and binds existence into a whole.*

And then he is gone.

"That's gotta be hard," says a thin young man with a blue do-rag tied around his head.

Good Directions

Friday morning after breakfast we wind through Tisbury and Chilmark. Stone walls, oak and white pine line the road. We make a right at Menemsha Road, snake uphill, admiring private homes tucked into niches. Night Heron Lane, foreshadowing the least bittern, comes up quickly.

We turn left and continue climbing. Bending over the map on her iPhone, Carol points to the unsigned road on our right flanked by huckleberry, bayberry and white oak saplings. I remember directions the Fisher King gave Parzival from his skiff—to make his first left and then continue across a bridge.

"This must be it," Carol's voice is hushed. "The entrance to *Ardetta Exilis*."

I make the left between imposing stone pillars 8 feet high onto a graded gravel road that curves gently up a wooded slope, noting that left is the direction of the unconscious, the side *sinister*. We pass a grassy alcove bordered by rhododendrons, then a Japanese garden featuring a pond surrounded by weeping cherry trees. We've entered a domain tended by precise and prosperous hands.

What appears to be a Mayan stele rises where the road loops right. We get out of the car and walk over. This stele is made of translucent polymer material. Words engraved on it turn out to be two four-line stanzas that ask us to consider which is most frightening, *an indifferent or hostile universe.*

"One of his," I tell her.

I'd been touched by the unornamented severity of Justin's memoir. The same quality in his poems chilled me at times. Skill and intelligence were evident. Imagination, less so. I follow Carol to a bench beneath the weeping cherry tree and I fill her in as best I can, starting with details I recall from his memoir.

Justin's mother was born in Hell's Kitchen. Her family owned a bucket-of-blood bar on Broadway, where the Irish mob known as the Westies hung out. Her brother had been a passionate fisherman. He took a bullet in a gang hit. She met her future husband, a charter boat captain, at her brother's wake. After their wedding, she moved to Sag Harbor, close to her husband's boat in Montauk. Photos in the memoir show Justin alone on the porch of a white house framed by potato fields, astride his bicycle, or in front of the boat. Hands that once dispensed chum, the smelly stew of fish parts, bones and blood thrown into the water as bait, now held a British passport and the key to rooms at Magdalen College.

"A long way from the south fork to the Menemsha Hills."

"For sure," remarked Carol.

I'd often fished out of Montauk on party boats. Except for excursions with my father, charters were financially out of my reach. It's possible that Justin and I crossed paths as teenagers on the dock. I spent enough time in that world to imagine what it was like to grow up as he did and why he felt compelled to escape it.

Less familiar is the world in which he now lives.

BE WELCOME HERE

The road ends at a parking area where a weathered woman in denim coveralls, her silver hair piled on her head, waves us into a parking space. Her dark eyes are wide-set above broad cheeks. It's hard to judge her age, but it is north of 40. She introduces herself as Lisa, then welcomes us to *Ardetta Exilis*.

"Any trouble finding us? First-timers often do."

"It's beautiful," observes Carol.

"What's left of our ancestral lands."

A full-blooded Wampanoag, Lisa tells us she traces her line back to the great chief Massasoit. With her coiled silver hair, even in work clothes, I think of her as a "princess." She helps us secure our backpacks, then carries our bags that flattens into a field bounded by a forest. We follow her to a gray cape perched on a deck that offers a view of the ocean trough a tangle of windswept pines. Lisa draws our attention to the Aquinnah cliffs.

"This is the highest point on the island," she tells us. "Over 300 feet."

Our princess opens the sliding glass door. The appointments inside the rustic exterior include brass bathroom fixtures, comforters stuffed with down and flower arrangements flanking silver trays of dried fruits and trail mix. Lisa encourages us to explore the grounds or rest. The path that follows the ocean leads to the Main House. Our host is expecting us for dinner at 8:30 p.m.

"Please," Lisa adds before taking her leave, "try to be on time."

Los Ultimos Rayos Del Sol

We start out early. The path runs through a bonsai forest of pines, limbs dwarfed and twisted by strong winds. Parallel rows of solar footlights line the gravel path across the lawn like a miniature landing strip. The lawn slopes west to a ridge. We walk to the edge. A steep descent drops to a beach carpeted with round stones 60 feet below. The Aquinnah Cliffs burn red in the last rays of the sun.

Carol points out a steep descent along a trail fringed by bayberry bushes. On the west side of the slope, white oak saplings flank a trail to a lookout, and from there the stairway leads to the beach. Small waves break soundlessly. A red-tailed hawk circles above them. Carol would like to go down there, feel the spray.

I touch my watch. "No time."

Last light spills over the bluffs like blood from the wound in a darkening sky. Before the sun disappears, we head back to the path. Solar lights come to life in the falling light and end at a wooden footbridge. On the other side, the Main House, a two-story hybrid sits on the crest of a rise surrounded by a blue-tile patio reminiscent of a moat. The first story is a fortress-like wall of weathered gray shingles set with cathedral windows over a recessed entrance. Above it, the second story, is a bank of tinted glass.

"*Ardetta Exiles*," whispers Carol.

Inside the Gothic niche, we approach carved oak doors.

"It's an eyrie," Carol squeezes my hand. "*Ardetta Exiles*: the bittern's nest."

"*The Fisherman Sent Me Here.*"

Failing to find a bell, I reach for the brass knocker shaped like an eagle's claw. Before I can bring it down, the door opens. The man facing us wears a navy cashmere crewneck over white ducks and boat shoes. I barely recognize him from the black-and-white photos in his memoir. His once-curly locks have thinned, turned reddish and threaded with gray. Parzival's first words at the castle gate cross my mind: "The fisherman sent me here."

"Welcome." Justin bows slightly, then stands back to let us in.

"I believe we're on time." I enter, with Carol close behind me.

"Perfect." His voice is soft, almost apologetic. "Forgive me. We keep only a small staff, so I must answer the door myself."

He is slightly bent like a question mark, until he straightens to his full height. I guess at 6-foot-3 or thereabouts. His head is large, even for a man of that size. We shake hands. I note that his are almost delicate, in contrast to his corded neck common to certain thin men whose muscles are like cables. More arresting still, his clean shaven face is unlined, except for grooves bracketing his mouth. His blue-grey eyes catch mine like fishhooks, then release me.

"Please." Justin takes our jackets, folds, then places them on a bench. When he leads us into the vestibule, I note a slight limp, as if one leg were a millimeter shorter than the other. He pauses on front of an abstract painting.

"de Kooning?" I guess.

"Auerbach," Justin corrects me. "Our greatest living painter."

We stop again in front of a cubist assemblage on a pedestal. Steel straps wrap a green vertical chessboard. I picture it in a garden by a wading pool, a New Age sundial.

"David Smith?"

Justin whispers. "It's a Caro.

Chamber Music."

"*Caro nome...*" says my wife.

"Ah, Rigoletto." His face lights up for a moment, then becomes stern. "I mean Anthony Caro. If you listen closely, this sculpture sings."

Head of E.O.W., Frank Auerbach, 1955

"Really?" My wife is fascinated.

"Not an aria, from the heart, but structural, like the vibration of a planetary ring. *Uranian* music." Justin steeples his fingers in front of his lips.

"How interesting," Carol is thoughtful.

Justin takes her arm. In front of the assemblage, he says, "Bend closer."

She fixes her attention. "It's like being inside a chambered nautilus."

He lets go of her arm. "Caro made this piece in the '60s. I found it in his studio last year before his death at 89."

We cross the threshold into a dimly lit room. Windows on the far side frame the night sky, which appears to be inside the room. Justin turns up the lights. The space bursts into color.

Paintings and weavings float on white walls, glazed ceramics glow on shelves and sculptures swim in niches luminous as reef fish. A monumental Anselm Kiefer dominates one wall with its mottled surface, lattices of blacks and golds floating like clouds in a white-and-blue sky above a field of wild flowers and mountains on the horizon. Carol and I have long admired Kiefer, a giant among contemporary German painters, as the visual biographer of the horror and guilt that haunts the postwar German soul. This canvas displays a sculptural topography of ridges and charged particles with the suggestion of train tracks. They must lead to Auschwitz.

"*Jerusalem*." Justin utters the title with a tilt of his monumental head.

I'm about to respond to such an equivalency, Jerusalem = Auschwitz, but our host has already disappeared through an arched doorway into the next room with my wife in tow.

A Seat at the Banquet

There are three steps leading down into the dining room. Justin cautions us to be careful. I note again his limp. He walks to the head of a table surrounded by 12 cathedral-back chairs. Tonight, it is set for four. Seated at the head, Justin indicates the chair on his right for Carol, the one to his left for me. Each place is set with delft china and Waterford crystal.

I'm drawn to a painting on the wall behind Carol, a beefy young woman, dark hair pinned back, a single toe-shoe peeking out of her white satin dress, her left arm plunged into a black boot she polishes with the cloth in her right. Moonlight through a window behind her floods the room with shadows. A cat stands on two legs under it looking up at the sky.

"What do you think?" Justin follows my gaze.

Balthus, Delvaux and Magritte…but know it's none of them.

"Paula Rego," he continues. "*The Policeman's Daughter*."

Rego, we learn, is Portuguese but resides in the U.K. She has been honored by the Queen. Justin knows Dame Paula. He describes her work as dominated by grotesque fairy-tale figures in narratives that hint at sexual secrets.

A statuesque, expensively preserved woman in her 50s interrupts our host when she enters from the kitchen through a door to my left. Her salt-and-pepper hair cut boyishly

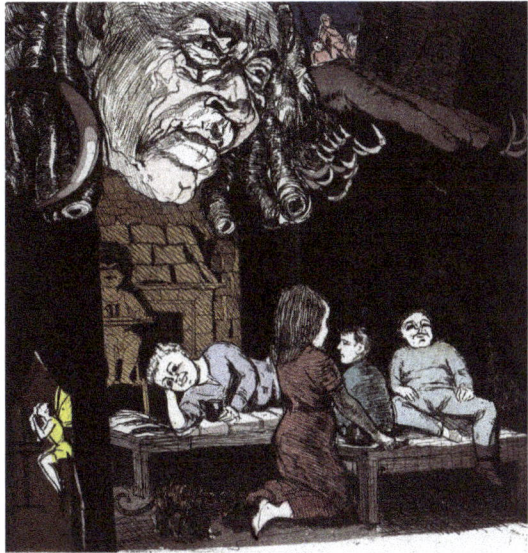

House Underground, Paula Rego

close frames a face defined by "good bones," webbed with fine lines. A white cardigan over designer jeans relieves her presentation without cheapening it.

"Good evening. So glad you could come."

"Violette, my fourth wife." Justin rises briefly.

"I hope you're not vegetarians." Her voice is slightly accented.

"Violette is French, more precisely, Parisian."

"I wouldn't have guessed," Carol told her.

"All those years at the American School," Violette replies.

"And Cornell," comments her husband.

"I'm a vet. Large animals. Mostly horses." She pours claret from a crystal decanter beside her husband, then moves to the opposite end of the table. "I hope you like daube."

"Beef stew, followed by port to seal the deal." Justin toasts, "*Bon appetit.*"

Carol observes that Justin seems to know the painters on display personally. "He makes a point of it." Violette rings the bell at her end.

Lisa, the Wampanoag princess, emerges from the kitchen wearing a white shirt and black pants, carrying daube in a silver tureen. She places the tureen in front of Justin, beside a stack of porcelain bowls. The smell of vegetables and meat seasoned with *herbes de Provence* fills the room when our host removes the lid.

Deliberately, as if peeling skin from a grape, Justin serves dinner. I ask him about Anselm Kiefer.

Justin shakes his head. Kiefer has become complacent. Rego continues working despite health issues. Frank Auerbach, he continues, is the genius of our time. He is productive at 85—and uninterested in the marketplace though his work increases in value by the day.

"The marketplace has been good to you," I observe.

"People I do business with know me." His blue-gray eyes take me in. "As we speak, I'm letting go of a company I built years ago to create a new one."

"Almost casually?"

"Exactly. It pays for the art. And for my other great love, the sea."

"One we share."

Justin is quick to let me know that here, too, I'm out of my depth. He's crossed the Atlantic in small crafts three times—most recently on the 38-footer, with two other men. He will make the next one alone.

"Tomorrow morning I'm sailing solo to Naushon Island in Buzzards Bay."

"A good life," I observe.

"Not without its challenges." A shadow passes over him.

"He's referring to his son and third wife." Violette, wife number four, talks openly. "And others who will go unnamed."

"Many depend on me. I take care of them." His voice changes. "I care *for* them, but not *about* them."

"Really?" Carol is piqued.

"I don't get emotionally involved."

Justin declares that he doesn't trust emotion, which includes love, vows of all kinds, gratitude and promises.

"What do you trust?" Carol asks him.

"The human need for protection. I provide this for others. After I'm gone, that ends."

"What do you mean?" Carol presses him.

"Tell them," Violette's frown lines deepen. She continues: "He's leaving all his wealth, including his art, to charity—nothing to his son who has not lived up to his expectations."

James Ensor: Self Portrait (detail)

"It must b e difficult to live up to the expectations of a father who has accomplished so much." I keep my tone neutral.

"Children of men like me don't fare well."

His tone is flat, but something flickers. I glimpse the Montauk bait boy who spent his childhood cleaning other people's fish. I wonder if we'd passed each other on the dock as kids, and if we had, would I have remembered him?

Violette rings the bell. Lisa, almost invisible in her ministrations, clears the table, then helps Violette serve fruit compote in crystal bowls. Our host pours red port into four snifters to go with the dessert, then turns his attention to Carol.

"You know *Caro nome*…?"

"I'm a voice teacher." She sings a few words from Gilda's aria in *Rigoletto*.

When Justin probes further, Carol describes her early career as a soloist with the original Wolf Trap Company and in Bernstein's *Mass*.

He listens closely when Carol confides that she'd found a professional career too stressful and, instead, taught public-school music until five years ago, when she opened her private voice studio.

Justin touches Carol's hand, then sings in a light, but not unmusical baritone:

> *La ci darem la mano,*
> *La mi dirai di si,*
> *Vedi, non e lontano,*
> *Partiam, ben mio, da qui.*

Carol responds in her haunting soprano:

> *Vorrei e non vorrei,*
> *Mi trema un poco il cor.*
> *Felice, e ver, sarei,*
> *Ma puo burlarmi ancor.*

"Mozart. *Don Giovanni*," says Justin.

"He attempts to seduce Zerlina," Carol explains. "*La ci darem la mano,* 'We will take each other's hands.'"

"My favorite duet." Justin half-sings the words. "'*Andiam, andiam*…come, come with me and reawaken the pleasure of innocent love.'"

Justin's long fingers linger on her wrist, before he withdraws them. But not his gaze.

"It doesn't end well for the Don," my wife continues. "He refuses to repent, and a chorus of demons take him down to hell."

"The baritone is undone." Justin apologizes. "As you can see, my greatest passion is opera."

"I thought you didn't trust emotion?" Carol reminds him.

"I'm not sentimental." Justin glances at his wife, then at mine. "But I have powerful desires."

"My very own Don Giovanni," Violette gazes at her husband, before her voice falls to a whisper. "And he, too, is unrepentant."

In that bait-boy voice, his eyes still fixed on Carol, he confesses to being a great philanderer. "It's the only thing I learned from my father, besides how to fish and captain a boat."

"I'm sorry about that," Carol stiffens and moves away.

"A question for you." I intervene.

"All right." Reluctantly, Justin turns toward me.

"Do you consider your impact on others?"

"What do you mean?"

"Your entire presentation from the moment we walked in has been a demonstration of your power. And now you sing Don Giovanni to my wife as if you're about to invoke the *droit de seigneur.*"

Justin appears surprised but recovers in seconds. A smile crosses his face. "Of course," he replies. "You could read it that way."

"Was it hard to meet your father's expectations?"

"I forgot, you're a psychotherapist." Justin nods. "I did everything he asked of me on the boat—cook, mate, rigger and fisherman. My father thought that everything else had little value, including my wealth, art or intellectual achievement. What you have seen here, my 'presentation' as you put it, would have meant nothing to him."

I suspect that his father's rejection of what others consider his son's accomplishments devalues them for Justin. I want to ask: *What ails thee?* But it would read here more like an indictment than a healing question. He has triggered my aggression rather than my compassion. Although ashamed, I am defiant. I'm also aware I may have missed an opportunity.

After coffee, I fold my napkin and place it beside the empty bowl. Carol pushes back her chair, thanks our hosts and wishes them a warm goodbye.

"Au revoir," says Violette. "I'm going riding in the morning and probably won't have a chance to see you."

We exchange European ghost kisses, then prepare to leave.

"A few more minutes of your time, please." Justin faces us. "I know you're tired. It won't take long. There's something I want to show you."

Floundering in the Underworld

A new note of urgency in his voice stops us. Violette and Princess Lisa have already started clearing the table. We follow Justin into another wing of the house, through corridors displaying artwork by blue-chip painters, sculptors and ceramicists, to a railed balcony shaped like the fantail of the ship from which I once watched a storm rage in the middle of the Pacific. This one looks down at the floor below. We descend single file on a spiral staircase a few feet away. I'm thinking of the unrepentant Don Giovanni sinking into hell surrounded by a chorus of demons and half-fear what we might find—the dead Don's corpse or a living Don's playground. I imagine a dungeon outfitted with leather whips and electronic sex toys.

But I am wrong.

The space resembles a cathedral—not through any architectural intention, but in the almost shrine-like arrangement of contents beneath a vaulted ceiling. State-of-the-art Bose speakers like icons stand in wall niches. Amplifiers, monitors and support equipment are ready to be summoned. At the center of the circular room, without windows or mirrors, a black leather chair waits with open arms like a throne on a carpeted platform. It is the circle squared. He wants to show us his temenos, where he feels safe and, perhaps, whole.

Carol and I have been given an audience in this throne room surrounded by invisible courtiers—tenors, baritones, sopranos and mezzos cloaked in CDs and vinyl, arranged in tiers of shelves like rungs on a heavenly ladder. The throne is placed optimally for balanced sound, can swivel or be adjusted for comfort at any angle of repose. There is a headset on the seat next to a remote.

Everything here, he confides, exists for him alone. He felt compelled to bring us here because of Carol. Her *Caro nome,* their duet *La ci darem la mano* ... the delicacy of her Zerlina to his Don Giovanni ... he let his explanation trail off.

I suspect it is an incomplete one. My question, however awkwardly, had pierced the shield of his wealth to rekindle his struggle with the Charter Boat Captain, the philandering father, who saw in his son only what he despised in himself.

It's the wound we share. How else could I have seen it in him?

"I am happiest here," he tells us. "I don't need anyone else. Let the world do what the world does, as long as I can sit in that chair and listen to Maria Callas."

Justin mounts the platform and picks up the remote. At first, I think that he will click the remote and fill the room with Callas, or Sutherland, another divine soprano.

"Imagine hearing Rosa Ponselle sing *Senza Mamma* at her piano at Villa Pace."

Carol utters: "*Oh, child, dying without your mother.*" Then sings: "*Senza mamma, o bimbo, tu sei morto!*"

We wait in anticipation of such an extraordinary operatic moment. The pause lengthens.

Something stirs in the depths of Justin's blue eyes, a sudden gravity pulls at his eyebrows, cheeks and mouth—then is replaced by an ironic smile.

"It's getting late. You must be tired," he steps awkwardly down from the throne. "And I must make an early start tomorrow in time to catch the tide."

The evening has come to an end. We have heard none of his music. It is abrupt, but final.

It is unclear why he has taken us this far only to stop short of sharing it. On the other hand, I might've asked to hear Rosa Ponselle sing *Senza Mamma* before he shut down. *Why didn't I?* I'm haunted by this on our way up the circular stair. It was an opportunity to change everything, and I missed it.

"Safe journey," Justin says as we retrieve our jackets in the vestibule. Then, with a slight nod of his head, he closes the door behind us.

Reeling It In

Packed and ready to leave *Ardetta Exiles* at 7 a.m., we walk to the Main House hoping to say goodbye. No one answers my claw-hammer knock. Justin told us that he'd be leaving early to catch the tide. We'd hoped to see Violette before she went riding. Back in the parking lot, we search for the Wampanoag princess to thank her for making us feel at home. But she is nowhere in evidence. Only the conifers stir in a sea breeze.

Belted into our Hyundai, Carol at the wheel, we start back along the road on which we arrived the day before. I remember the silence that surrounded Parzival on the morning after his banquet. He'd raced through the empty rooms and corridors calling out to those who had served him the day before and received no response. Unlike the abandoned knight, we do not, as Wolfram puts it, "burst into a passion of grief and anger." But I can't honestly say that we are completely free of those emotions.

Justin protested that his solitude is sufficient. For all of his material abundance, he remains sealed in his chamber, unable to share his suffering that continues on his solitary operatic frequency unheard. Then I remember my own silence during that awkward interval before he ended the evening, during which I might've asked to hear his music—his ironic smile.

"Why are you frowning?" asks Carol.

"What if the Fisher King were to become like the neutrino, a particle that leaves no footprint but binds the world?"

"Not sure where you're going with this."

"I really blew it. I should have asked to hear his music."

"Most of us miss that moment. It goes by too fast." She slows passing the weeping cherries. "Think you can stop punishing yourself?"

"Probably not."

We salute Justin's default question engraved in polymer: *What frightens us most, the indifference or hostility of the universe?*

DANCING IN THE END ZONE

Clam chowder in Styrofoam bowls tastes especially good on the top deck of the *M/V Island Home.* At Woods Hole, I take the wheel. The silence is comforting as we cross Buzzard's Bay on the Bourne Bridge, each of us attending the theaters of our own minds. At the end of the Mass Pike, we enter New York State.

After so much time in New England, Albany looks unkempt as we approach it from the east side of the Hudson River.

The capital of New York State is a bizarre assemblage of architectural periods, the archaeological remains of an in-

Everything is Permitted, Wayne Atherton

coherent culture. Rockefeller's modernist Empire State Plaza, with its three phallic white tombstones and the otherworldly entertainment center. Then—19th century row houses are interspersed by Gothic and ...like the State Capital.

"Home again," I observe.

"Ready for re-entry?"

"I'm working on it."

"Your missed opportunity with Justin?"

She asks me again to let go of it, then challenges my conclusion, tells me that we did get through to him. When I express doubt, Carol insists she saw something in his eyes when she sang *O bimbo, tu sei morto.*

"What?"

131

Melancholia (detail), Albrecht Durer

"A motherless child," she said.

"I still should have asked to hear his music."

It was my Parzival moment. We would never return to that castle again. Maybe we don't have to. This is the way the tale ends at this moment in time: The glimpse is everything. I say as much to Carol. She agrees.

"Where does that leave us?" I ask her.

"Personally, I'm looking forward to poached salmon and a glass of wine." She yawns. "Then early to bed."

"We'll open a bottle of Breca," I tell her.

We turn right at Albany on the elevated loop that crosses the Hudson to merge with 787 North, along the river to Troy. I redirect Parzival's question, *What ails me?*

The answer, I conclude, is *numbness.*

"Stay to the right," my wife directs me. "We turn off here."

"I see it."

"What are you feeling?" she asks.

"Lost," I tell her.

"Let's stop at the supermarket," says Carol. "We need salad, vegetables and a baguette."

I wait in the car, my head down. The last thing I am prepared to handle is an old student telling me how much she appreciated my mythology course. Especially *Parzival.*

What if your wound went unaddressed for 10 centuries? A voice I haven't heard for days comes as a shock and a relief.

"So much has changed," I agree.

Except the will to change.

"Not change," I challenge Pedrolino. "Massive disruption. We have no image for who we are or where we find ourselves."

Stuck on Ra's boat, in the fifth hour.

"A boat full of ghosts."

And only the seabirds to keep chaos at bay.

"Maybe I can't see the Fisher King's face because he has none."

So, we troll.

"Beyond imagination."

Then how do you explain me? Pedrolino drives his point home by falling silent.

Carol returns with two bags of groceries. She is surprised to find me smiling.

"While you were shopping, I had an epiphany." I tell her.

"Care to share it?" She slips into the passenger's seat.

"The imagination has a voice."

I explain that like most people I thought of the imagination as the source of imagery, but now understand that even when there is no image it acts as a voice to bring things to light.

"It speaks to me more often these days."

"What does it tell you?"

I quote Charles Olson. "*As the dead prey on us, /they are the dead in ourselves, /awake my sleeping ones, I cry/ out to you, / disentangle the nets of being!*"

She touches my cheek.

Unbidden, I hear another voice, one I recognize as belonging to John Cleese calling out in *Monty Python and the Holy Grail* from the faux battlements to himself as Lancelot: *Sacre bleu! What a wise ass.*

A few minutes later we pull into our driveway in front of the white ranch on our tree-lined street in Glens Falls, New York, home of Bob and Ray's "Slow Talkers of America." Juggling groceries, I take comfort in this and in "quantum uncertainty" that suggests a particle can exist everywhere and nowhere, until consciousness connects subject to object and we see as we are seen. I see that the Fisher King wound can be expressed as the Abraxas/Pauli constant that connects the atoms to the stars.

SUMMONING THE
WORLD SOUL

Splendor Solis - "Arma Artis"

At the end of a great symphony or when you've listened to a great poem there's often nothing to say. You're being pushed beyond rational thoughts and distinctions into a silent intuitive space.

Karen Armstrong

THE WOUND AND THE WORLD SOUL

Wolfram's figure of the Fisher King emerged in the first quarter of the 13th century as part of a changing world order. Those returning to Europe from the Crusades brought back with them ideas, attitudes and information which were the fruits of the Islamic Golden Age that began in the 8th and extended into the 13th century, during which scholars translated Greco-Roman works of classical antiquity covering medicine, mathematics and philosophy. Before the first knights landed in the Holy Land, Arab scholars like Avicenna debated the ideas of Plato, Plotinus and Aristotle with his colleagues and speculated on the notion of self-awareness in a thought experiment he called "the Floating Man," which posited that under extreme sense deprivation a person would remain aware of his existence.

A weave of new ideas emerged during the Renaissance in the Hermetic writings of Marsilio Ficino, Pico della Mirandola and Giordano Bruno and continued in the procession of 17th century philosopher/alchemists. Wolfram conceived of the Holy Grail as a virtual Philosopher's Stone. He describes the *lapis exillis* as a "super jewel surpassing in its powers." *Parzival* weaves symbols from Celtic/Christian traditions in drawing on the mythical sixth-century British king, Arthur, who mounted a defense against invading Saxons. Wolfram reshaped this legend found in Geoffrey of Monmouth's pseudohistorical *History of the British Kings* (1139), into the one we have come to know. In *Parzival,* Chivalry is an ethos in decline, ritualized killing that has produced a Wasteland. Pursuit of the Grail as a symbol of hope at a time of suffering makes it clear that redemption is possible only through a change in consciousness. The Fisher King in his skiff can be compared to Avicenna's Floating Man in the sensory deprivation chamber, steeped in self-awareness. The unfolding narrative of *Parzival* is a nuanced exploration of consciousness, rising from the unconscious, as the wound that contains its own cure.

THE FLOATING MAN

Robert Johnson, in his book, *The Fisher King and the Handless Maiden,* argues that our culture suffers from a wounded feeling function. As he indicates, "feeling," as he is using that word, is neither sensation nor emotion, but the connection to what Plato in the *Timaeus* calls "… a living being endowed with a soul and intelligence … containing all other living entities," and what the 16th-century physician/alchemist Gerhard Dorn refers to as the World Soul *(anima mundi)*. Hegel speaks of it as the *Geist*, an intelligence that not only contains the record of our collective history, but also responds to it. The philosopher Alfred North Whitehead suggests the World Soul has two components, the unchanging primordial and the contextual one that shares our suffering and joy. The Primordial abides but is informed by the contextual experience of the other unfolding in space-time. Physicist Erwin Schrodinger tells us: "The total number of minds in the universe is one. In fact, consciousness is a singularity phasing within all beings."

Embracing the Universe, Roy Lawaetz

Our various forms of woundedness inform the World Soul that suffers with us.

The World Soul, in turn, pins us to the production of symbols, myths and dreams formed in its primordial aspect and which emerge in its consequent one. These don't always flow in sympathy with our condition. At times the flow goes underground. Details blur. Symbols age, lose power and all but vanish from sight. But even when we aren't able to access a clearly imagined symbolic form, the connection to it exists as what Jung called an "imperishable element of the unconscious." The Fisher King may no longer sit across from us at the banquet table, but we can still try to locate the *Fisher King Function* in that which pierces through to touch our wound as an act of love.

UNDRESSING THE WOUND

The *Fisher King Function* raises the issue of the "cure-in-the-disease." This idea—that "like cures like" or that what causes the disease may, in small doses, cure it—is found in most folk medicines around the world. It is said that Hippocrates in 400 B.C.E. prescribed small doses of mandrake root to treat mania, knowing that in larger doses it produces mania. Edward Jenner discovered in 1796 that scratching the skin with a solution of cowpox virus inoculated the body against the full-blown smallpox. As controversial as it has become, homeopathy is defined as "the treatment of disease by minute doses of natural substances that in a healthy person would produce symptoms of disease."

When Amfortas returned to the castle after killing his adversary, physicians removed the iron head and wooden splinter of the shaft that wounded him from his groin. But the wound would not heal. None of the many remedies tried brought relief—not a piece of the golden bough that ushered Aeneas into the Underworld, nor the blood of the pelican that wounds itself to feed its young, nor the unicorn's heart. It became evident that the movement of the stars, orbiting planets, constella-

Achilles scrapes rust into Telephus' wound, Herculaneum

139

tions and phases of the moon affected the wound. When Saturn brought the summer snow, Amfortas' caretakers inserted the hot spear tip of the lance, re- wounding him. Only the tip applied to the wound drew "the frost from his body." The direct application of the wounding agent to the wound can be linked to the *pharmakon*, which is both poison and cure, discussed in Plato's *Phaedrus*. Both Plato and Hippocrates were followers of Asclepius, who healed through dreams.

Perhaps the earliest instance of a direct application of the weapon as cure to the wound it created occurs in the myth of Achilles and Telephus. On their way to Troy, Achilles wounded Telephus, king of Mysias, in the thigh. The wound would not heal, and the Greeks were uncertain of the course to Troy. Achilles heard that Telephus could show them the way to Troy if his wound was cured by the one who wounded him. Achilles effected the healing by scraping rust from his spear directly into Telephus' wound.

The idea of sympathetic healing, which appears to have first been expressed by Apollo's oracle, could as easily have emerged from an Asclepian dream incubator. By the 17th century, physicians based this practice on the notion that Man and the Universe were composed of a common substance, analogous to Dorn's World Soul. This substance demonstrates the equivalent of what in quantum mechanics is called "complementarity," the interchangeable nature of matter and energy; accordingly, the relationship of weapon to wound evolved into the sword-salve controversy.

SWORD AND SALVE

The 16th-century Swiss doctor Paracelsus, father of herbal and psychosomatic medicine, built his practice on his observation that in nature the cure of a disease could be extracted from its cause. The pseudo-Paracelsian book *Archidoxis Magica*, written by his followers and published in 1570, introduced the notion of the Weapon Salve. The premise was that a salve could be made to cure a wound from blood residue on the weapon that inflicted it. The salve, applied to the weapon, might work through *sympathy* among elements to heal the wound at a distance. By the 17th century, on the threshold of the Enlightenment, the Sword-Salve controversy had become a hot-button issue.

Many found the notion absurd. They charged that physical contact was essential to causation. Religious conservatives called the idea demonic. Theosophists, on the other hand, pointed to the new study of magnetism as proof that objects could be moved without physical contact. Alchemist and physician Robert Fludd adhered to the argument that this was possible through the animating energy of the World Soul.

Normally, healing begins when the weapon is separated from the wound. In this narrative, weapon and wound create a field that collapses time, space and causality. Weapon and wound are inseparable, even over a distance. Their synergy creates a single vector through which healing takes place. Psychologically speaking, healing through reconnecting with the wound is central to depth psychology and trauma theory as this form of treatment has evolved from Freud and Jung. I might say that the repair of the world depends on it.

UBI SUNT

Jung tells us, "The archetypes are imperishable elements of the unconscious, but they change their shape continually." (CW9i) Absent the mythic imagery, we gaze into the abyss. Without archetypal landmarks, we are lost at sea. The impact of post-internet culture on these *imperishable elements of the unconscious* is uncertain. Perhaps the universe, which we learn looks more to us like a mind than a machine, has begun to reimagine itself. The shapes that once connected us to the imperishable may now be seated inside us as memories or manifest as psychosomatic disorders. We search for the salve that heals at a distance. Maybe in the vacuum left by our old idea, a new one will become visible. We let out the imaginary lines of our daily lives in search of even a glimpse of it, hoping to reel in something that will explain the unexplainable. I recall that moment in the Bahamas when

I saw the Divine Child in the marlin's eye before it disappeared back into the primordial depths—and feel a cry rising from my own darkness to meet that memory: *What good is this, unless something is born from it, seed of my heartbreak?*

SUMMONING THE WORLD SOUL

Gerhard Dorn suggested that it was God who must be redeemed by man through the transformation of his conflicted consciousness. Dorn's *Speculative Philosophy* (1567) describes the alchemical opus as inner work in which that split is healed. He may have used an arcane language, but the condition, and its consequences, remain compelling in any language. The wound calls out to us, whether or not we hear it.

The irascible Paracelsus—credited with founding toxicology, diagnosing psychosomatic disease, applying antiseptics, treating pain with laudanum, arteriosclerosis with highly toxic black hellebore (Hippocrates' purgative) and poor blood with iron—was also regarded as a lout, a drunkard prone to explosive outbursts of abusive language who burned the works of Aristotle in a bonfire, along with those of Avicenna and Galen and led "a legion of homicidal physicians." Little wonder that such a walking contradiction should believe that the cure of a disease could be extracted from its cause.

The hunger to find a unitary principle was common to alchemists/physicians like Paracelsus and Dorn who envisioned repairing the conflict in themselves and nature by producing a Marriage of Opposites. As Monika Wikman writes in *Pregnant Darkness*, "Alchemists such as Gerhard Dorn, in his work 'The Speculative Philosophy,' referred to this next alchemical stage [inner healing] as *Unus Mundus*, where splits are healed, duality ceases and the individual, the *vir unus*, unites with the world soul." Think of physicist Wolfgang Pauli's despair before the problem posed by the anomalous Zeeman Effect or Einstein's frustrating search for the unified field as a single sacred fish.

As I reflected on these questions, a prose poem by Major Regain, a professor who teaches at Kent State University in Ohio, arrived as an email attachment. It recounted his conversation over coffee with a former colleague at the Brady Café. His friend, a lifelong muskie fisherman, describes his encounter with a legendary muskie, rumored to be "as long as a boat oar," in the West Branch of the Reservoir, near Ravenna. Every fall, this fisherman had gathered his gear and hunted him. Last October, the muskie came out of a weed bed east of the dam and followed the fisherman's lure to the boat, then suddenly "sank under the hull" and shot out "like a torpedo that missed its target." I understand how the fisherman felt, sitting with his fishing rod across his knees trying to make sense of what had just happened to him. In that moment, I stood beside him holding my childhood rig. Major's words reached me over an imponderable distance as though he were at my side.

"An old Hasidic teaching sees demons, spirits residing in all objects, all things. The work is to release the powers resident in matter. This leads to an understanding of all acts as sacramental."

REIMAGINING THE WOUND

Apollo Mask, Phidias, 5th Century. B.C.E.

The Fisher King as I'd imagined him has fallen silent. I am willing to accept the possibility that he no longer exists, but I hold firm to the perpetuity of the wound, that it is elsewhere embodied as the dismembered mother at the heart of creation who cries out for reparations.

At the end of the day, I can't turn my back on the figure in the black hoodie or my presence beside him holding my childhood rig. The dream may have been asking me

143

to reconsider the essential questions from another point of view, one more consistent with the later stage of life. On the other hand, there may be a clarity that can be viewed only through a child's eyes. Or both. The figure beside me hidden from view, his body bent like a living question mark, might well have belonged to any of the PTSD vets returning from Vietnam, Iraq or Afghanistan. The moral wound so many suffer in explosive moments, or utter numbness, can look like that.

I had always seen Amfortas and his wound as a child might, assumed the story required his healing on the way to a happy ending. It occurs to me now that a deeper meaning might lie in the courage to bear the wound rather than heal it. The hooded figure will not speak, or meet my eyes, because he can't. It isn't his intention to shun me. His presence, however, has opened my ears to a voice that protests "our nullification." In the absence of an image, I listen for that voice, a mystery that is all and nothing, an invisible particle that holds the material world together but leaves no footprint. I locate its source as the skiff in my heart afloat where the world's wounds wash the shores of desire at immeasurable depth.

THE SECRET AT THE CENTER OF STONES: THE 'FISHER KING FUNCTION.'

Stone #1

The Grail, Wolfram tells us, is a stone, the *lapis exillis*. Lit from within, it glows like a precious jewel with an iridescence that begs description. Neutral angels removed the Grail from the warring angels in heaven by bringing it to safety below. They placed it under the protection of mortals whose devotion to it was unquestioned until Amfortas, the Fisher King, on the wings of youthful passion, violated his oath and imperiled his mission. Under the banner of Amor, in the name of love, he took the life of another knight in battle and sustained a wound that wouldn't heal. The object he had pledged to protect, the stone that drew its energy from the Anima Mundi, became orphaned and at the same time attached to its former keeper's wound, a disruption in the natural order and in the psychological one.

Rhine, Stella Waitzkin

While the failure to sustain that order resulted in distress to both, the properties of the stone itself remained active. The intelligence it expressed originated within the stone. Messages that appeared on its surface disappeared to make room for others. As in dreams, what they conveyed seemed oracular and intentional. Then there was the amplitude of its gifts, food sufficient to feed a banquet and maintain the entire court at the Grail Castle. In this respect, like the quantum universe, it resembled a mind rather than a mechanical device and provided refuge for the lineage of Grail Keepers past, present and future. The Grail mingled the traits of angels and mortals, and so stood with respect to them both in accord and in antithesis to its own mystery.

Stone #2

Charles Olson also refers to a mysterious stone at the opening of Part 2 of "The Kingfishers," *I thought of the E on the stone.*

As Plutarch tells it in his essay "The Obsolescence of Oracles," Zeus launched two eagles flying at the same speed from opposite ends of the earth and dropped a stone from the point at which they met. It landed at Delphi on a spot that was henceforth considered to be the center of the world—the omphalos, "Earth's navel." Olson references this stone.

According to Ralph Maud, Olson was reading Plutarch's "On the E at Delphi" while composing "The Kingfishers." In the essay, Plutarch, a priest of Apollo for his last 30 years, discussed the possible meaning of the fifth letter in the Greek alphabet carved into that stone. Five is a powerful number. It denotes Plato's five perfect shapes in nature, the five elements and the five senses. It is also the word for "if," and the second-person singular of the verb to be: "thou art." By the end of the essay, Plutarch was forced to admit that the exact meaning of the E is unknowable, except as a message that mingles the joy of the gods with mortal sorrow. Even so, in Plutarch's words, the renowned words carved into the Temple's lintel, KNOW THYSELF, "seem to stand in a sort of antithesis to the letter 'E', and yet, again, to accord with it."

What might Olson have been thinking as he considered the imaginary stone?

From this point of view, the admonition to KNOW THYSELF is a starting point, not the goal. "The Kingfishers" is an interrogation of knowledge at odds with itself and the self that seeks it—the very symbol systems that anchored both, now adrift in the world. Olson casts his net of questions to capture the vestiges of what had been connected, the shapes and artifacts of displaced orders. Like the Grail, the E on the Delphic stone mingles joy and sorrow, and demands to be reconciled.

Olson's pursuit betrays nostalgia for a center that holds: for the missing matrix, a reliable omphalos. It is a search for what might change the attitude of his historical moment, address what he has discerned as the missing piece to the puzzle: *to KNOW THYSELF requires a connection to something that knows the knower.* In Wolfram's mythos, Parzival becomes precisely that to the Fisher King.

The Goal

There is something suggestive about the intelligence at the center of stones—which are primordial artifacts of the creation. If the imaginal representation of stones points to something unimaginable, it is the possibility of a vital intelligence at their *silent center,* evidence of immortal joy and mortal sorrow in the mineral womb. It may be interesting to note that the great world traveler of the classical world, Pausanias, described the omphalos at Delphi a century after Plutarch as surrounded by precious stones in the shape of mermaids—which more closely resembles Wolfram's *lapis exilis.*

The question remains: What can these stones tell us about our longing to penetrate to the center of a condition mingling the gods' joy with mortal sorrow?

In *Memories, Dreams and Reflections,* C.G. Jung recounts a dream in which he finds himself in "Liverpool," a dark, sooty city, among a group of Swiss tourists. They make their way to a park overlooking the world below. It is configured like a mandala, and Jung finds himself at the center facing a circular fountain. In the middle of the fountain stands a magnolia tree with a shower of reddish blossoms in a halo of sunlight. The area surrounding this remains dim, foggy, and opaque. The others complain about the dreariness of the landscape, oblivious of Jung's experience. Jung understands that the revelation of the center that has been there all along is what has made it possible for him to exist in this "pool of life." This center has always been the goal: the omphalos. Circumambulating his unconscious, he wakes to the apprehension of "something that knows the knower." Jung's journey resonates in this respect with Wolfram's, Parzival's and Olson's.

In all three narratives, a common theme is the obliviousness of others to the pain of their condition. Those at the party in "The Kingfishers" shrug off the polluted center, the pool full of slime. Jung's Swiss companions in "Liverpool" speak of the abominable weather as he basks in the beauty of the sunlit tree. Parzival is blind to the Wasteland of his war-torn landscape.

The elusive but desired goal appears to exist consubstantially in another dimension, but tantalizingly close enough to ignite our longing for what Sallust in the first century B.C.E. points to as that which "never came into existence because it always is."

The Fisher King Function

Synesius of Cyrene (370-415 A.D.) in a *Treatise on Dreams*, tells us that "pain cleanses the soul of ignorant joy." Hence, clarity, and the fruits thereof, can only be attained through cleansing pain. One can only imagine what is left after the cleansing, another kind of joy, a deep knowing—the goal of the Fisher King wound.

Our culture is driven by the desire to avoid pain at any cost. In denying the reality of suffering, as Viktor Frankel points out, we create a vacuum filled by the will to pleasure and to power—the apotheosis of ignorant joy. *Man's Search for Meaning* is Frankel's love letter to suffering, which he affirms is essential to the full realization of our humanity. Fortunately, what has fallen silent in our waking experience continues to exist in our dreams. Wolfram, Olson and Jung testify that there is no shortcut to the goal, and that in an age of numbing distraction and accelerated change, it is harder than ever to hear what calls to us through time, the voice of the open heart at the end of a tortuous course.

To this end, I propose reimagining the wound.

Parzival and Amfortas no longer exist as identifiable objects of knowledge outside of us. We have internalized them as functions, which languish when not addressed. Like the other gods we've ingested, they become body aches and diseases. We infect the planet and our politics with our desperation to disconnect from the pain that invites us to the banquet.

Under these circumstances, I see no alternative to the necessity of embracing what I call the *Fisher King Function*, to consciously abide with/in the pain that cleanses ignorant joy and to circumambulate the terror raging in the battleground of life's unfolding, until we find the silent center. Jung has revealed this as a process of deep change inherent in the course of individuation, guided by what he calls "The Transcendent Function." What I am alluding to is a more operational emphasis in the day-to-day arena, a way of re-educating the culture at every level.

The idea is to change the way we think about trauma, anger, grief and anxiety as antagonists to be subdued, and instead understand them as messengers with important information, the writing that appears and disappears on the surface of the Grail, revelations of the Amfortas wound. The *Fisher King Function* will guide us to the objects of our primal intuition, the sunlit tree at the center of the mandala, the face that was hidden in the hoodie, something that knows the knower, finally, as known.

NOTES

NOTE ONE: DISENTANGLING THE NETS

The opening two sections of Charles Olson's "The Kingfishers."
The complete poem can be accessed at THE POETRY FOUNDATION,

https://www.poetryfoundation.org/poems-and-poets/poems/detail/
54310

The Kingfishers –
by CHARLES OLSON

1

What does not change / is the will to change

He woke, fully clothed, in his bed. He
remembered only one thing, the birds, how
when he came in, he had gone around the rooms
and got them back in their cage, the green one first, s
he with the bad leg, and then the blue,
the one they had hoped was a male

Otherwise? Yes, Fernand, who had talked lispingly of Albers
& Angkor Vat. He had left the party without a word.
How he got up, got into his coat, I do not know.
When I saw him, he was at the door, but it did not matter,
he was already sliding along the wall of the night, losing himself
in some crack of the ruins. That it should have been he who
said, "The kingfishers! who caresfor their feathers now?"

His last words had been, "The pool is slime." Suddenly everyone,
ceasing their talk, sat in a row around him, watched

they did not so much hear, or pay attention, they
wondered, looked at each other, smirked, but listened,
he repeated and repeated, could not go beyond his thought
"The pool the kingfishers' feathers were wealth why
did the export stop?"

It was then he left

2

I thought of the E on the stone, and of what Mao said
la lumiere"
                but the kingfisher
de l'aurore"
                but the kingfisher flew west
est devant nous!
                he got the color of his breast
                from the heat of the setting sun!

The features are, the feebleness of the feet (syndactylism of the
3rd & 4th digit)
the bill, serrated, sometimes a pronounced beak, the wings
where the color is, short and round, the tail inconspicuous.

But not these things were the factors. Not the birds.
The legends are
legends. Dead, hung up indoors, the kingfisher
will not indicate a favoring wind,
or avert the thunderbolt. Nor, by its nesting,
still the waters, with the new year, for seven days.
It is true, it does nest with the opening year, but not on the
waters. It nests at the end of a tunnel bored by itself in a bank.
There, six or eight white and translucent eggs are laid, on
fishbones not on bare clay, on bones thrown up in pellets by
the birds.

On these rejectamenta
(as they accumulate they form a cup-shaped structure) the
young are born.
And, as they are fed and grow, this nest of excrement and
decayed fish becomes
          a dripping, fetid mass

Mao concluded:
    nous devons
        nous lever
           et agir!

Charles Olson, "The Kingfishers" from *The Collected Poems of Charles Olson*. Copyright © 1987 by the Regents of the University of California. Reprinted with the permission of University of California Press.
    Source: *The Collected Poems of Charles Olson* (University of California Press, 1987)

NOTE TWO: THE WORLD CLOCK

From *Synchronicity* by F. David Peat

The World Clock. An impression generated by artist W. Beyers-Brown
based on accounts of Pauli's dream.

David Peat describes the physical characteristics of the clock following Jung's in his book, *Psychology and Alchemy.*

There is a vertical and a horizontal circle, having a common center. This is the world clock. It is supported by the blackbird.

The vertical circle is a blue disc with a white border divided into 4 by 8—32 partitions. A pointer rotates upon it.

The horizontal circle consists of four colors. On it stand four little men with pendulums, and around it is laid the ring that was once dark and is now golden (formerly carried by four children). The world clock has three rhythms or pulses:

The small pulse: the pointer on the blue vertical disc advances by 1/32.

The middle pulse: one complete rotation of the pointer. At the same time the horizontal circle advances by 1/32.

The great pulse: 32 middle pulses are equal to one complete rotation of the golden ring. (p. 194)

…Jung identified the point of rotation of the disks with the mystical speculum, *for it both partakes of the rhythmic movement yet stands outside it. The two disks belong to the two universes of the conscious and the unconscious, which intersect in this speculum. The whole figure together with its elaborate internal movement is therefore a mandala of the Self, which is at one and the same time the center and the periphery of the world clock. In addition, the dream could also stand as a model of the universe itself and the nature of space-time…*

Wolfgang Pauli and the Fine-Structure Constant

By Michael A. Sherbon

Journal of Science (JOS) 148 Vol. 2, No. 3, 2012, ISSN 2324-9854 Copyright © World Science Publisher, United States www.worldsciencepublisher.org

"Another interpretation of Pauli's World Clock could be made comparing it to a basic yin-yang space-time model of brain-mind function describing hemispheric interactions [13]. Pauli associated the rhythms of the World Clock with biological processes (in particular the four chambers of the heart and its average rhythm of 72 beats per minute) as well as with psychic processes [14]. In Wolfgang Pauli's visionary World Clock geometry the blackbird is a symbol for the "turning inward" at the beginning stage of alchemy and the messenger for the creative solar principle."

Pauli & Jung: The Meeting of Two Great Minds

By David Lindorff

Following the dream of "The House of Gathering," Pauli experienced a waking vision that came to him with great clarity and left him with the feeling of "Sublime harmony." He called it "The Great Vision." The Text reads ... "This vision of two cosmic clocks orthogonally related to each other by a common center challenges our rational prejudice as we contemplate the physical unrealizability of the construction of The World Clock. The image is a three dimensional mandala symbolically representing the structure of space and time, which have a common center point".

The empty center shows that there is no Deity within the symbol. Taking the vision to have collective significance, Jung observed that modern humans have the task of relating to the whole person, or the self, rather than to a god-image that is a projection of the self."

NOTE THREE: THE FLOATING MAN

JACK LONDON & THE FLOATING MAN

The idea that proof of the independent existence of consciousness, or the soul, is explored at length in Jack London's novel *The Sea Wolf*. Like many writing at the start of the 20th century, London was fascinated by Social Darwinism as a way of accounting for the disparities between the rich and poor, powerful and weak—and at the same time drawn to the social ideals of Marx and a family of workers. These opposing viewpoints extended to the materialist/idealist controversy. He articulated both the Darwinian and Materialist point of view through the Captain of *The Ghost,* Wolf Larsen, an autodidact isolated on the ship he commands until he rescues a literary critic, Humphrey, after a ferry has overturned between Oakland and San Francisco. Larsen attempts to convince Hump that might is right in argument and by subjecting him to harsh treatment to toughen him up. Life for Wolf is essentially meaningless beyond this, and infinitely replaceable. Hump resists. When Maud Brewster, a castaway, is taken on board, Hump becomes her protector. They fall in love and, emboldened by their alliance, attempt to convince Wolf that there is a soul, which exists independent of the body. What ensues is a long Platonic argument along these lines that ends when the three of them are shipwrecked together, and Wolf suffers a heart attack. He first goes blind, then his right side becomes paralyzed, and later, his other arm and leg. Finally, his voice goes. Before he loses his last connection to the physical world, Wolf is able to indicate that he is still alive inside, and whatever it is that registers life is independent of the physical body. The parallels to Avicenna's floating man and the wounded Fisher King/Parzival might be discussed at length at another time.

NOTE FOUR: SWORD-SALVE

The Original Myth: ACHILLES AND TELEPHUS

Telephus, son of Heracles and Auge, was a king in Asia Minor. After nearly making the same mistake as Oedipus, of marrying his own mother, Telephus married a daughter of King Priam. As an ally of the Trojans, his kingdom was attacked by the Greeks (or Achaeans) and in the fighting Telephus was wounded in the thigh by the spear of Achilles. After the Greeks had withdrawn, Telephus' wound would not heal.

The Greeks had no leader who could show them the way to Troy. But Telephus, because his wound was unhealed--[the oracle of] Apollo had told him that he would be cured when the one who wounded him should turn physician--came from Mysia to Argos, clad in rags, and begged the help of Achilles, promising to show the course to steer for Troy. So Achilles healed him by scraping off the rust of his Pelian spear. Accordingly, on being healed, Telephus showed the course to steer, and the accuracy of his information was confirmed by Calchas by means of his own art of divination.

[Apollodorus, tr. Sir James George Frazer]

Posts Tagged 'Royal Society of London'
Most of the information here about the salve/sword controversy and healing practices is taken from: Isseicreekphilosophy's Blog Sympathetic Magic, the Weapon Salve and the Powder of Sympathy in the 17th Century

Nearly a hundred years after Paracelsus' death in 1541, a few of his followers suggested a protocol that involved curing a wound with the weapon that caused it. It was based on the principle well known to practitioners of sympathetic and homeopathic medicine that the cure was secreted in the cause of the disease. They claimed that blood and other residue from the weapon that inflicted the wound might be compounded into a salve to heal the wound it had inflicted.

Moreover, the salve could do this by being applied to the weapon, rather than to the wound itself.

Paracelsus passed down the protocol as follows:

Take of moss growing on the head of a thief who has been hanged and left in the air; of real mummy; of human blood, still warm – of each one ounce; of human suet, two ounces; of linseed oil, turpentine, and Armenian bole – of each two drachms. Mix all well in a mortar, and keep the salve in an oblong, narrow urn.

The argument over the efficacy of the treatment divided prominent thinkers of the time, especially in England. Paracelsian proponents like Robert Fludd, John Baptista von Helmont and Sir Kenelm Digby faced spirited opposition in figures like Clergyman William Foster and Daniel Sennert.

Taken literally, the notion for many was absurd. William Foster presented his essay as a sponge "to wipe away the Weapon-Salve, wherein is proved that the Cure taken up among us by applying the Salve to the Weapon is magical and unlawful" (1629 and 1641).

Philosopher/physician Robert Fludd responds in *The Squezing of Parson Foster's Sponge* that the alignment of sympathetic micro- and macro-cosmic energies made this form of healing possible. "This explains how there is no impediment or stops of the spirit from being conveyed through the air even if there is a corporeal body in between."

Foster insisted the cure could not be found in the Bible and was therefore demonic and, like any other witch's spell, could as easily by the same laws be used to kill the patient. Moreover, no such thing could happen over a distance, without a causative agent.

Fludd countered that the spirit of the blood may be transferred from the body to the anointed weapon just as the magnetic force can draw separate parts together over an unlimited distance.

Dr. Daniel Sennert argued forcibly that the magnetism of the lodestone works only over short distances and in a straight line. The weapon salve as evidence of cosmic magnetism is an occult science.

Foster questioned the credibility of the cure's progenitor, Paracelsus, a man who "…endevored to bring many strange and un-heard of practices into the Art of Medicine, [and] that he was a man of base and wicked life and conversation."

This argument reminds me of one raised in quantum physics about the interface between particle and wave and the mirroring behavior of particles over a distance without any visible causative agent. Einstein referred to this entanglement as "spooky action at a distance" and remained uncomfortable with it as an unexplained phenomenon.

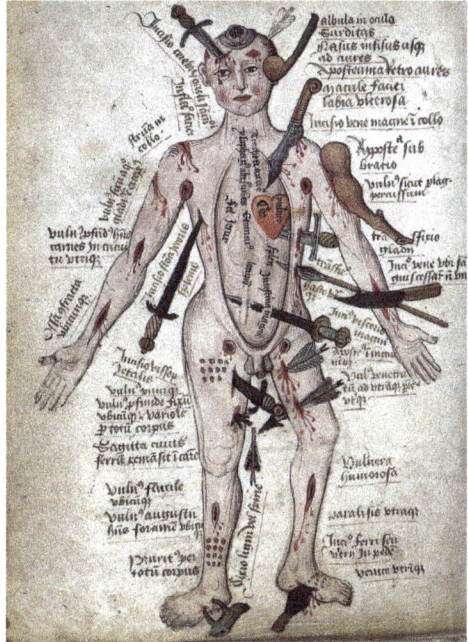

The Wound Man-Wellcome Library

"The pseudo-Paracelsian text *Archidoxis Magica* lists the ingredients for this curative salve as well as the manner in which the salve should be prepared as follows: Take of that Moss which grows upon a skull or a bone of a dead body that has lain in the air, of man's grease, of mummy, and man's blood, linseed oil, oil of roses and bole- armoniack, and '[l]et them all beat together in a Morter so long, until they come to a most pure and subtil [*sic*] Oyntment; then keep it in a Box,' and when someone gets wounded, you are to dip a wooden stick in the blood so it would become bloody. Upon drying the blood, thrust it in the ointment, and leave it for a while. Afterwards, you are to 'binde up the wound with a new Linen Rowler, every morning washing it with the Patients own Urine; and it shall be healed, be it never so great, without any Plaister or Pain.' The author of this Paracelsian text tells us that "you may cure any one that is wounded, though he be ten miles distant from you, if you have but his blood."

Isseicreekphilosophy's blog

https://isseicreekphilosophy.wordpress.com/2012/04/28/sympathetic-magic-the-weapon-salve-and-the-powder-of-sympathy-in-the-17th-century-europe/

NOTE FIVE: JESUS AND THE MUSKIE

Saturday, 92-degree heat, the first hot, heavy day of summer. The Brady Café, late morning coffee. A faculty guy from the local university sits down at my table, smoking cup in hand. He tells me he has been away in a treatment center for an oil change and tune-up, a scouring of the brain pan. He says, *I met three or four guys each of whom thought he was Jesus. Every day they expected the Second Coming. Their daily proclamation was that they were going to save the world. They never said how. They were convinced the world had it wrong; they had it right. But, hey, everybody in there thought that, not just the Messiahs. The strange thing was not one of them knew about the others. I knew about all of them. Because I found out about them, they saw me as an Antichrist, the Beast. I counted the days till I was discharged.*

He gazes out the window as the hump and stutter of traffic picks up. *You know I'm a muskie fisherman, have been all my life. Over in the West Branch Reservoir, near Ravenna, there is a huge muskie, long as a boat oar, who lurks in a thick weeded bed east of the dam. Everybody knows about him. Every fall I hunt him. Last October, he followed my lure right up to the boat, then sank out of sight under the hull, like a torpedo that missed its target and churned on to God knows where. I just sat there a long time with my fishing rod across my knees. It was some kind of visitation. My brother tells me those big muskie eat only once a day. Everything else is out of anger, pure meanness.*

He is retired and gone from town now, moved south to milder winters. I'll not forget him, this man who knew four Jesuses and believed in a muskie as tall as St. John of the Cross. An old Hasidic teaching sees demons, spirits residing in all objects, all things. The work is to release the powers resident in matter. This leads to an understanding of all acts as sacramental.

Major Ragain

ILLUSTRATIONS:

COVER: 15th Cen. St. Brenden & the stranded whale, British Museum, https://commons.wikimedia.org/wiki/File:Baleine_Harley_3244.jpg, Public Domain

CHAPTER I: ADDRESSING THE WOUND

1) The Sleep of Arthur in Avalon (Detail) - https://commons.wikimedia.org/wiki/File:Edward_Burne-Jones. The_last_sleep_of_Arthur.jpg
2) War Interrupted, Wayne Atherton-permission from the artist
3) Screen Man, Marc Shanker-permission from the artist

CHAPTER II: DISENTANGLING THE NET

2) Splendor Solis – the Dark Sun, https://commons.wikimedia.org/wiki/File:Splendor_Solis_19_ dark_sun.jpg Public Domain
3) Vincent Ferrini, (monoprint) by Jain Tarnower @ The Gloucester Writers Center permission from the artist
4) Mounting The Bounty - Wayne Atherton-permission from the artist
5) Kingfisher hovering, iStock, Close up of a Common Kingfisher (Alcedo Atthis)
6) Ra on the sun barque with the Bennu Bird, iStockphoto, Egyptian Gods

THE ARCHEOLOGY OF DREAMS

7) Crossing the River Styx—from the collection of Paul & Carol Pines
8) The Wounded Fisher King, http://www.forrester-roberts.co.uk/fisher_king.html
9) Swordfish, Brunetto Latini's Livre de Tresor, Public Domain
10) Nick's Diner, By Flickr user: Jim Kuhn Takoma Park http://www.flickr.com/people/takomabibelot/ [CC BY 2.0 (http://creativecommons.org/licenses/by/2.0)], via Wikimedia Commons

CONSTELLATING THE NET: A QUANTUM FIARYTALE

11) The Spiritual Pilgrim Discovering Another World, 17th Century, By Heikenwaelder Hugo, Austria, Email: heikenwaelder@aon.at, www.heikenwaelder.at [CC BY-SA 2.5 (http://creativecommons.org/licenses/by-sa/2.5)], via Wikimedia Commons

12) Fish Map #3, Wayne Atherton—with permission of the artist

13) Angelus Novus, Paul Klee [Public domain], via Wikimedia Commons

14) Bohr's Model Atom, Illustration by Danijela Mijailovic

15) Robert Fludd Utriusque cosmi maioris scilicet et minoris... (1619) [Public domain], via Wikimedia Commons

16) Wolfgang Pauli: Photo of Wolfgang Pauli by Nobel foundation [Public domain], via Wikimedia Commons https://commons.wikimedia.org/wiki/File:Pauli.jpg. Illustration by Danijela Mijailovic

BIBLIOGRAPHY

ACZEL, D. Amir, Entanglement, *The Greatest Mystery in Physics*, New York: Four Walls Eight Windows, 2001

AUGUSTINE, of Hippo, *The Confessions of St. Augustine*, Forgotten Books, 2016 BATESON, G. (1979), *Mind and Nature: A Necessary Unity, (Advances in Systems Theory, Complexity, and the Human Sciences)*. Hampton Press

BUDGE, Wallis, E.A., *The Gods of the Egyptians*, Vols 1 & 2, Dover, NY, 1969 CAMPBELL, Joseph, *The Hero with A Thousand Faces*, Princeton/Bollingen, N.J. 1949

_____ with Bill MOYERS, *The Power of Myth*, Doubleday, NY, 1988

_____ with Michael TOMS, *An Open Life*, Harper&Row, NY 1990 CLARKE, Lindsay, *Parzival, and the Stone from Heaven*, Thorsons, London, 2001

CORBETT, Lionel, *The Sacred Cauldron*, Chiron Publications, Il, 2014

DANIELSON, Dennis Richard ed., *The Book of The Cosmos, Imagining the Universe from Heraclitus to Hawking*, New York: Perseus Publishing, 2000

DE TROYES, Chretien, *Perceval*, tr. Burton RAFFEL, Yale University Press, CT, 1999

EINSTEIN, Albert, *Cosmic Religion: With Other Opinions and Aphorisms*, New York, Covici-Freide, 1931

EDINGER, Edward, *Ego and Archetype*, New York: Putnam, 1972 FERRINI, Vincent, *Know Fish*, University of Connecticut Library, CT, 1979

GELL-MANN, Murray, *The Quark and the Jaguar, Adventures in the Simple and Complex*, San Francisco, W.H. Freeman, 1994

HILLMAN, James, *Re-Visioning Psychology*, New York, Harper Paperbacks, 1977

_____, *The Soul's Code, In Search of Character and Calling*, New York, Grand Central Publishing, 1997

_____, *Lament of the Dead, Psychology after Jung's RED BOOK*, with Sonu Shamdasani, NY, W.W. Norton, 2013

HEGEL, G.W.F., *Hegel's Preface to the Phenomenology of Spirit*, translated with introduction, running commentary and notes by Yirmiyahu Yovel, Princeton: Princeton University Press, 2004

HOLLIS, James, *Mythologems, Incarnations of the Invisible World*, Toronto, Inner City Books, 2004

_____, *Under Saturn's Shadow*, Inner City Books, Toronto, 1994

_____, *The Eden Project*, Inner City Books, Toronto, 1998

HORNUNG, Erik, tr, David Lorton, *The Ancient Egyptian Books of the Afterlife*, Cornell University Press, CT, 1997

JAMES, William, *The Principles of Psychology, vol 1*, New York, Cosimo Classics, 2007 JOHNSON, Robert, A., *The Fisher King and the Handless Maiden*, S.F., Harpercollins, 1993

JUNG, C.G. *The Collected Works*, (Bollingen Series XX) 20 vol. Trans. R.C.F. Hull. Ed. H.

Read, Princeton University Press, 1953-79

_____, *Man and his Symbols*, New York Doubleday and Co., 1964

_____, *Memories, Dreams, Reflection*, Ed. Aniela Jaffe, New York, Pantheon Books, 1961

_____, *Commentary of 'The Secret of the Golden Flower'*, 1957. In Alchemical Studies, vol. 13, The Collected Works of C.G. Jung. Princeton, NJ: Princeton University Press, 1967

_____, *The Red Book; Liber Novus*, Edited and introduced by Sonu Shamdasani. New York, W.W. Norton, 2009

JUNG, C.G., *Dream Interpretation Ancient and Modern*, ed. John PECK, Princeton University Press, NJ 2014

JUNG, C.G., and Wolfgang PAULI, *Atom and Archetype: The Pauli-Jung Letters 1932-1958*, Edited by C.A. Meier, Princeton, NJ; Princeton University Press, 2001

JUNG, Emma and M.L. VON FRANZ, *The Grail Legend*, Sigo Press, Boston, 1980

LINDORFF, David, Jung and Pauli, Quest Books, Wheaton, Il, 2004

MATTHEWS, John, *King Arthur and the Grail Quest*, Brockhampton Press, London, 1995 MAUD, Ralph, *The Significance of Charles Olson's "The Kingfishers,"* Fairleigh Dickenson University Press, Teaneck, 1988

Bibliography

MILLER, Arthur, I., *137: Jung, Pauli and the Pursuit of a Scientific Obsession*, W.W. Norton, NY 2009

NIETZSCHE Friedrich, *The Portable Nietzsche*, Ed. Walter Kaufman, New York, Viking, 1972 OLSON, Charles, *Archeologist of Morning*, Cape Goliard, London, 1970

Maximus, Cape Goliard, London, 1968

PEAT, F. David. *Synchronicity: The Bridge Between Matter and Mind*, New York: Bantam, 1987

_____, *Infinite Potential, The Life and Times of David Bohm*, MA., Addison-Wesley, 1997 PINES, Paul, *My Brother's Madness*, Curbstone Press, CT 2007

_____, *The Tin Angel*, Wm. Morrow, NY, 1965

PLATO, _____ *Plato's Phaedrus*, ed. R. Hackforth, The Library of the Liberal Arts, NY, 1952 _____ *The Republic*

SCHWEITZER, Andreas, *The Sun God's Journey through the Netherworld*, Cornell University Press, CT, 1999

SALMAN, Sherry, *Dreams of Totality*, Spring Journal Books, New Orleans, Louisiana, 2013 STEWART, Mary, *The Crystal Cave*, Harper Collins, NY, 1970

_____ *The Hollow Hills*, Harper Collins, NY, 1973

_____ *The Last Enchantment*, Harper Collins, NY, 1980

TODD, Peter B., *The Individuation of God, Integrating Science and Religion*, Ill, Chiron Publications, 2012

TWAIN, Mark, *A Connecticut Yankee in King Arthur's Court*, Dover, NY 2001 Von ESCHENBACH, Wolfram, *Parzival*, New York, Vintage Books, 1961

Von FRANZ, Marie-Louise, *Alchemical Active Imagination*, Shambhala, Boston, 1997

WAITE, A.E., *The Holy Grail*, University Books, NY, 1961 WHITE, E.B., *The Once and Future King*, Berkley, NY 1965 WICKMAN, Monica, *Pregnant Darkness*, Nicholas-Hays, 2004

WHITMONT, C. Edward, *The Alchemy of Healing: Psyche and Soma*, CA, North Atlantic Books, 1993

YATES, Frances A., *The Art of Memory*, Chicago: University of Chicago Press, 1966

COMMENTS ON OTHER BOOKS BY PAUL PINES

MY BROTHER'S MADNESS

My Brother's Madness is part thriller, part an exploration that not only describes the causes, character, and journey of mental illness, but also makes sense of it. It is ultimately a story of our own humanity.   —*Kirkus Reviews*

Take what pain, hope, sorrow, and madness there is in this world, pass it through the alembic of an educated sensibility and a deep, informed compassion, and you might be lucky enough to reach *My Brother's Madness*. — James Hollis, Jungian Analyst, and author of *Why Good People do Bad Things*

My Brother's Madness ...emerges as a triumph in behavioral science literature...   — Dr. Jared Ritter, *Psychiatric Services, a Journal of the American Psychiatric Association*

THE TIN ANGEL

This swift tale of murder and revenge rattled along stylishly and fulfills all our expectations for high-grade suspense.   —*The New York Times Book Review.*

Superb...enough terror, suspense, and low-life atmosphere to keep the most jaded hard-boiled enthusiast happy.   —*The Washington Post*

I haven't read a grittier mystery in years, or—I suspect—a truer one. — *NY Daily News*

THE HOTEL MADDEN POEMS

Hotel Madden is a fine and powerful book.   —William Bronk

Paul Pines' dedication to *Hotel Madden Poems* describes the book as a "fugue." That's exactly what this brilliant and compelling work is...   — Lawrence Joseph, *American Book Review*

BREATH

...the Poems in *Breath* constitute a heartfelt, extended meditation on the transporting effects of everyday phenomena, how the psychic wormholes that allow instantaneous travel along our internal galaxies hide just underneath the next memory, the next sentence, and behind the all, the ALL itself— unknowable, perhaps, but in Pines' poetry nearly imaginable.   — Fred Muratori, *The American Book review*

Comments on other Books by Paul Pines

ADRIFT ON BLINDING LIGHT

Pines takes the reader on a mysterious, complicated journey. Dreams, archetypes, icons, friends, and confessions swirl through the poems in beautiful and complex images. ... This wonderfully unpredictable, intuitive book navigates the conscious and subconscious worlds with fluid, imaginative, and fascinating energy— as poets should do.　　— William Kelly, *Multicultural Review*

Adrift on Blinding Light is full of exquisite moments; of words and phrases that have been mined by the author like gems and presented to us with the sense of wonder they engender and deserve.　　— Lee Bellavance, *The Café Review*

TAXIDANCING

Reading Pines is not unlike listening to good jazz. The poems are strangely emblematic, allowing us to progressively come into their world, becoming, as we go, increasingly hip and eager to hear their urgencies.　　— Julia Conner, *First Intensity*

What a background for a poet. Paul Pines grew up in Brooklyn and spent time in the Lower East Side of NYC. He tended bar, drove a cab, shipped out as a merchant seaman, and opened his own jazz club in the Bowery, The Tin Palace, in 1970. He is now a practicing psychotherapist in upstate New York. So this ain't your usual MFA-trained bard, but certainly one who has been well-schooled. Hugely recommended.　　— Doug Holder, *Boston Area Small Press and Scene.*

LAST CALL AT THE TIN PALACE

Last Call at the Tin Palace, by Paul Pines...poems that are stories that are jazz that are memories that are everlasting imprints of music on retinas... — Bob Holman, *Poetry Picks*　　　　— *The Best Books of 2009*

Thank you, Paul Pines, for a sublime ride! — David Meltzer

...the poems are magical, revealing, yet personal, and all the time — engaging. *Last Call at the Tin Palace* delivers.　　— Brian Gilmore, *Jazz Times*

REFLECTIONS IN A SMOKING MIRROR

The only other person I can compare this to is Goethe. ... Powerful stuff!
— Paul Elisha, *NPR-WAMC*

These poems are similar to a Keith Jarret concert. They can rip your heart out and leave the reader defenseless.   — Doug Holder, *Boston Area Small Press and Scene.*

Merely stating that the book proved "insightful" doesn't do justice to the unexpected expansion of consciousness.   — *Jottings of an AmeriQuebeckian*

DIVINE MADNESS

Paul Pines' *Divine Madness*, an empathic scatting to the music of the spheres that seems to sound simultaneously from both the deepest interior of human consciousness and the farthest reach of the celestial dome.   —Fred Muratori, *The Notre Dame Review*

In modes as diverse as the crime novel (*The Tin Angel),* the memoir *(My Brother's Madness*), opera, and eight volumes of poetry, Pines pursues—with keen and nuanced observation—the psyche's flights, fissures, mania, and brilliance.   —Naftali Rottenstreich, *Big Bridge #17*

NEW ORLEANS VARIATIONS & PARIS OUROBOROS

...some of the most memorable and finely wrought poems of anybody on the scene today...   —Louis Proyect, *The Unrepentent Marxist*

His [Pines'] chiseled reveries are insightful yet affecting in their sheer presence...   —Burt Kimmelman, *Golden Handcuffs Review*

With his latest, Paul Pines reveals himself to be at the peak of his poetic powers...the movements across and between a multiplicity of references is just fabulous...the collection is a wonderful manifestation of something he quotes from Homer: "We leave home to find ourselves."   —Eileen Tabios, *Galatea Resurrects #21*

Comments on other Books by Paul Pines

FISHING ON THE POLE STAR

Paul Pines is a poet that communicates in a clear style information of an epic order...islands as destinations in a gnostic soul voyage. *Fishing On The Pole Star* is composed of short narratives within allegorical overlay...as crisp and cleanly presented as Hemmingway's *Old Man and the Sea*... —Donald Wellman, podcast at the *Gloucester Writers Center http://gloucesterwriters.org/ podcast/paul-pines/*

These poems, set in the Bahamas, are themselves fish swimming in the white ocean of the book's pages. The long thin island of Eleuthera is also represented in the concrete structure of the opening poem. ... This is a beautiful book, enhanced by stunning collage illustrations from the artist Wayne Atherton. —Stephen Wilson, *Jewish Quarterly, UK*

MESSAGE FROM THE MEMOIRIST

I've just come from a long dip in enriched waters authored by Paul Pines, *Message from the Memoirist*...For Pines, memory is a dynamic, a cauldron, a witching lure, a weeping and a singing. It is a final/final promise of being, becoming itself. He has written this book of poetry to celebrate that. —Ralph La Charity, *Galatea Resurrects*

Wolfgang Pauli, the famous physicist and pioneer of Quantum Theory, had a vision of The World Clock, a contraption of wheels and pendulums supported by a large black bird and emitting pulses. ... As the reader pages through Pines' provocative collection...it strikes one that these pieces and their intersecting memories make up a clock not unlike Pauli's. Remember to take the time (steal it if necessary), let this book unfold, and soak in the compelling and quantum landscapes of master poet Paul Pines. —Dennis Daly, *Boston Area Small Press and Poetry Scene*

CHARLOTTE SONGS

On the surface, this beautifully designed book has the touching qualities of a family album, interspersing with the text color snapshots of Charlotte in such guises as an insouciant-looking infant in the arms of her adoring father, a pre-teenager with a Dali moustache penciled on her upper lip, and an Ophelia playing dead upon a coffin.... Yet, as deceptively simple in their clear images and common speech as they are, these poems are songs sung from the heart of this poet: they transcend as well as embody the occasion. —David M. Katz, *Jewish Quarterly, UK.*

Trolling with the Fisher King

It was only when I realized how rare such tributes are that I began to understand the true importance of these spare, elegant poems. *Charlotte Songs* confronts head on the passionate, watchful father faced not with a lost or troubled daughter but with the ordinary tension that arises between a child, striving for independence, and a father trying to stave the loss that independence implies.　—Hasanthika Sirisena, *American Book Review*

AUTHOR BIO

PAUL PINES opened The Tin Palace, his Bowery jazz club, in the '70s. It became the setting for his novel *The Tin Angel* (Morrow, 1983). A second novel, *Redemption,* (Editions du Rocher, 1997), explores the Guatemalan Mayan genocide of the '80s. *My Brother's Madness,* (Curbstone Press, 2007) probes the nature of delusion. He has published 13 collections of poetry, most recently *Divine Madness* (Marsh Hawk, 2012), *Fishing On The Pole Star* (Dos Madres, 2014) *Message From The Memoirist* (Dos Madres, 2015) and *Charlotte Songs* (Marsh Hawk, 2016). He is the editor of Juan Gelman's selected poems *Dark Times/ Filled with Light* (Open Letters Press, 2012) and has contributed translations to *Small Hours of the Night, Selected Poems of Roque Dalton* and *Nicanor Parra, Antipoems: New and Selected.* Composer Daniel Asia's settings of Pines' poems appear on *Songs from the Page of Swords, Breath in a Ram's Horn* and *Purer Than Purest Pure* (BBC Singers) on the Summit label. Asia's *5th Symphony*, recorded by the Pilsen SO, features poems by Pines and Israeli poet Yehuda Amichai. *The Tin Angel Opera* was performed by the Center for Contemporary Opera in NYC.

Pines has conducted workshops for the National Writers Voice and lectured for the National Endowment for the Humanities. He has been a fellow at the MacDowell Colony, Ossabaw Foundation and Virginia Center, as well as a recipient of an Artists' Fellowship, N.Y.S. Foundation for the Arts. He lives in Glens Falls, New York, where he is a psychotherapist in private practice and hosts the Lake George Jazz Weekend.

paulpines.com
https://www.amazon.com/Paul-Pines/e/B001JOZNSA

www.ingramcontent.com/pod-product-compliance
Lightning Source LLC
Chambersburg PA
CBHW040141270326
41928CB00022B/3283